NEGOTIATING TOWARD TRUTH

The Extinction of Teachers and Students

VIBS

Volume 62

Robert Ginsberg
Executive Editor

Associate Editors

G. John M. Abbarno
Mary-Rose Barral
Virginia Black
H. G. Callaway
Rem B. Edwards
Rob Fisher
Dane R. Gordon
J. Everet Green
Heta Häyry
Matti Häyry
Richard T. Hull

Joseph C. Kunkel
Ruth M. Lucier
Alan Milchman
George David Miller
Michael H. Mitias
Samuel M. Natale
Peter A. Redpath
Alan Rosenberg
Arleen Salles
Alan Soble
Daniel Statman

A volume in
Philosophy of Education
PHED
George David Miller, Editor

NEGOTIATING TOWARD TRUTH

The Extinction of Teachers and Students

George David Miller

Rodopi

Amsterdam - Atlanta, GA 1998

Cover design by Chris Kok based on a photograph, ©1984 by Robert Ginsberg, of statuary by Gustav Vigeland in the Frogner Park, Oslo, Norway.

⊚ The paper on which this book is printed meets the requirements of "ISO 9706:1994, Information and documentation - Paper for documents - Requirements for permanence".

ISBN: 90-420-0268-9 (bound)
ISBN: 90-420-0258-1 (paper)
©Editions Rodopi B.V., Amsterdam - Atlanta, GA 1998
Printed in The Netherlands

If I were in charge of the world,
I'd cancel all alcoholic beverages, cigarettes, and also violence.

If I were in charge of the world,
There'd be equal opportunities, and equal amounts of
money for everyone.

If I were in charge of the world,
You wouldn't have any wars.
You wouldn't have any pollution.
You wouldn't have to die.
You wouldn't even have grades.

If I were in charge of the world,
All people
would be able to get a full education;
All people would be equal;
And persons who sometimes
couldn't be their best, and sometimes
didn't agree
Would still be allowed to be
 In charge of the world.

—Laura Miller

CONTENTS

FOREWORD

In *Negotiating Toward Truth*, George David Miller asks the right questions about education. Anyone concerned about the state of education today should read it.

And anyone reading it should be prepared for the answers Miller posits, for they are never squeamish or tepid. Just about everyone today has strong opinions regarding education in the United States. Most decry the current state of affairs. Whether from the left or right—from educators, students or laypersons—we know that something is not working. Without getting into a debate about how much worse things are today than in the past, Miller simply declares that the entire system needs to be thrown out. There is no baby in the bath water worth saving, as reformers would have it. Now, says Miller, is the time to throw whatever is in the bath water out with the water. Nobody gets off easily with Miller as he systematically moves his reader toward what must replace what gets thrown out: a pedagogy of dynamism. Like Martin Luther posting his Ninety-five Theses on the doors of Wittenberg's Castle Cathedral, Miller boldly states his forty-one "Dicta of a Radical Pedagogy of Dynamism."

No doubt Miller intends his manifesto to be as radicalizing as were Luther's Ninety-five Theses. From dictum number one, "Cosmic Dynamism: You can never piss in the same river," to number forty-one, "Truth is compatible, and only compatible, with radicalism," Miller takes philosophical positions based on the values he holds. Every dictum—all forty-one—is given a full-blown defense in the final chapter. Readers will be challenged by the time they get through them to think and rethink whatever educational philosophy they embrace—or to formulate one where none may exist.

The radical pedagogy of dynamism Miller finally asserts grows in large part from Paulo Freire's philosophy of being/becoming in his *Pedagogy of the Oppressed*. Miller's admiration for Freire's caring, love, and hope for the oppressed is sincerely unabashed. Miller argues that at the core of both Freire's philosophy and his own is understanding the teacher-student, student-teacher relationship. In coming to the pedagogical creed of the final chapter, Miller discusses, in separate chapters, two pivotal educational philosophers: John Dewey and Alfred North Whitehead. In still another chapter, he examines how Friedrich Nietzsche's philosophical thought in a number of his works has contributed indirectly to educational theory.

Whitehead and Dewey do not get off so easily. Both are systematically dissected, first Whitehead's reformist approach and next Dewey's shallowness. Although Miller gives each some credit for seeing what needs fixing, ultimately he concludes that neither could figure out how to fix it. In short, Whitehead misses the need for dialoguing about ideas, and Dewey misunderstands the nature of thinking.

Miller shapes his educational philosophy in a framework that many of today's deconstructionists, psychoanalysts, and relativists would find hard to accept. He affirms negotiation through dialoguing, creativity, fear of dynamism, and an increasing humanization of human beings. These values, and more, make up Miller's philosophy of dynamism. Every value is explored and re-explored against the backdrop of a panoply of philosophers while at every turn, Miller's aggressiveness and indignation come through in the passion of his arguments.

Given Miller's genuine commitment to asking the most difficult questions, I would argue that this manifesto pushes us to pose other questions: What exactly are the methods for enacting the radical philosophy of becoming espoused in this book? How can a value inquiry effect change beyond its impassioned rhetoric? How can educators learn to work from the desire of those being educated—to my mind, the only place where real change occurs? How can psychoanalytic theory push us toward understanding others from the inside out, not the outside in, as positivists do? How can radicals really dialogue when they seem to answer the question before it is asked? How much control do radicals exert in a learning setting, no matter what they proclaim about being a fellow learners? If radicals proclaim they openly "despise" reformers, how will they ever get reformers to listen to their answers? How do we know an oppressor when we see one? What causes inequality and unhappiness—only oppression? What other evils besides oppression exact harm upon others? What drives people to seek radical change? What drives them not to? Finally, what exactly is "becoming-being?"

No matter what hard questions readers may be stimulated to pose after reading this book, they cannot be neutral toward the ideas expressed here. I share here just a sampler: "Reformers are deformers," "Writing the birth announcement for philosophy means writing the obituary for religion," "Have respect for obscenity." All the old truisms are questioned, but more important than anything else in the book is Miller's emphasis on the value of love. For him, it is the central focus for forming a truly radical teacher-student relationship: "The ultimate loving relationship is one in which people simultaneously view one another as both teachers and students. . . . I contend that our fundamental ontological relationship with others is marked by loving." Herein lies Miller's ultimate challenge to the teacher.

Elaine Ross
English Department
Lewis University

ACKNOWLEDGMENTS

Without Norma Miller, there would be no text.

Norma told me again and again: "Please, George, please back up the text. The system might crash and then you would have nothing." I thought the chances of my system crashing were as remote as the Stock Market crashing again. So like the disobedient husband that I am, I refused to listen. Everything was going fine and I had only to cross a few t's and dot a few i's and then I would be finished. Only hours before I intended to send the manuscript to Robert Ginsberg, Executive Editor of the Value Inquiry Book Series, I came home from class and saw my wife sitting crestfallen at the computer. She told me the worst thing had just happened. Immediately, I thought about my children and the people who were closest to me. Teary-eyed, she told me that the computer crashed and everything was gone. I felt like the Joad family in *The Grapes of Wrath*, but I actually took it fairly well, only once running headlong toward the window. I ordered a pizza and commiserated with the delivery person about loss in general.

Fortunately, I found a hard copy of the text. Norma used a scanner at work, and I was back in business.

This is not the only episode like this in my life. Norma has seen lots more. But I want to let her know I appreciate her for saving me here and elsewhere.

INTRODUCTION

I am a radical and not a reformer.

Let me make that clear from the beginning.

Reformers are gradualists. Bit by bit, little by little, things will get better, they say. Evolution, not revolution, they say. Build on what we have, they say. Don't throw the baby out with the bath water, they say. That is only common sense.

Now is the time to throw whatever is in the bath water out with the bath water, I declare.

Now don't get the wrong idea. I'm not a baby hater, and I don't want to add to the already high infant mortality rate in our highly industrialized and civilized society. Reformers want you to believe there is a cute little baby in the bath water. That's why you wouldn't want to throw it out. Radicals want to tell you it's a beast, not a baby, in the water.

Radicals say: The whole system is rotten to the core and we must come up with a new system to replace it. Because what we have is rotten, we cannot build on it. The bath water's dirty because you have a putrid monster defecating in it. And a monster can only evolve into something more monstrous. Thus, throw the beast out with the bath water.

Radicalism is not simply a replacement of one inert system with another. Radicalism is a commitment to dynamism, to the growth and development of individual and social organisms. Radicalism advocates an organic and dynamic system.

Commitment is central to radicalism. Commitment means to be bound intellectually and emotionally, in word and in deed, to a course of action. Commitment is a primary value of radicalism. We might even say that radicalism is commitment to commitment.

Radicalism, then, has its roots in value. It values commitment, but a particular kind of commitment. Its commitment is to the value of persons and their development. If human beings are in process and their development depends upon creating and recreating their environments, then commitment to their well-being consists of cultivating their creativity. Creativity is another primary value of radicalism.

Radicalism is a commitment to our innate creativity. Radicalism affirms the innate creativity of human beings and trusts we can properly exercise our creativity for the purposes of self-determination. Creativity is not mere adaptation, simply reacting to the environment, a kind of self-defense. Creativity is the spontaneous initiation of change by human beings.

The commitment of radicalism to the development of person suggests concern for other human beings. This concern might be termed love or caring. Loving or caring represents another primary value of radicalism.

What are the optimal conditions for loving or caring? In the optimal conditions, can I say that I benefit others and others benefit me? How do I benefit others? By helping them develop themselves. How do others help me? By helping me develop myself.

In a loving or caring relationship, I open myself up to you. I trust you. You open yourself up to me. You trust me. We become receptive to one another. To what exactly are we being receptive? To another person's attempts to help us.

But a loving or caring relationship is not simply an opening up to another person. At the same time, loving or caring is aimed at helping another person. A loving or caring relationship is characterized by helping and allowing to be helped.

This is where the path twists a little. What does it mean to allow you to help me? Perhaps it means to allow you to teach me, to put me in the role of a learner. But you are not merely teaching me, but learning to teach me. I am not only learning from you, but am teaching you at the same time. If the loving or caring relationship means we meet as equals, this suggests that I am not a repository waiting to be filled by your knowledge and dominated by it. Instead, each of us is spontaneous and receptive. I am receptive to what you have to teach me, but never become a mere receptacle. For you, I am a being capable of my own spontaneity. I can teach. For me, you are not simply my benefactor, but someone who can benefit from me. You can learn.

Everybody is both teacher and student. As Paulo Freire says: "Education must begin with the solution of the teacher-student contradiction, by reconciling the poles of the contradiction so that both are simultaneously teachers *and* students."[1] I teach; therefore, I learn. I learn; therefore, I teach. Teaching and learning are not separate acts, but an integrated continuum.

To another related point: All human acts are teaching and learning. Our fundamental relationship with both the world and others is teaching-learning. A civilization recognizing these intuitions believes that every moment is one of teaching-learning. In everything, there is a lesson to be learned and taught.

This brings me to the stage of indicting the predominant pedagogy.

Why is the American system of education rotten to the core? I could point to student apathy. I could point to teacher ineffectiveness. I could point to consumerism. I could point to technology. I could point to a gross watering down of the curriculum. I could point to parents. I could point to capitalism. I could point to many of you and certainly myself, a co-conspirator in the system and one who has many times tried to throw out the bath water while preserving the baby.

The biggest problem in education is, coincidentally, the biggest problem in philosophy and also the biggest issue we have as human beings. This is the problem of being and becoming. For me, understanding being-becoming leads back to the examination of the nature of thinking itself. Perhaps a resolution of the being-becoming issue will allow us to create optimal conditions for loving or caring and for teaching and learning.

In "My Pedagogic Creed,"[2] John Dewey begins his philosophy of education by defining education. This is the wrong beginning. All inquiries about education (like all other inquiries) should begin with the question: what is a human being?

Human beings are often depicted as dichotomies. We are forever trying to secure a wholeness that is not possible. We are sinners trying to become saints. We are finite beings yearning to be infinite. We are between ignorance and knowledge. We are individual entities seeking to be one with the cosmos. Or, following Kant, we are both phenomenal and noumenal beings. Or, following Sartre, we pursue the impossible project of being both the for-itself and in-itself. We seek a wholeness that can never be ours. But the desire to become whole never leaves. That is our mark.

A clue to addressing this question, I believe, can be found in the writings of the ancient Greek philosopher, Heraclitus. Heraclitus supposedly said that you can't step in the same river twice. But he also said that logos runs through all things. The river represents becoming; logos, being. Human beings are part of the parade of becoming, no doubt. We are also intrinsically tied to being. Instead of saying that human beings are a dichotomy of being and becoming, we can say that we are an integration of being and becoming.

"Being" is often defined as "what is." Hegel believes that pure being excludes all distinctions and is no thing. Because it excludes every thing, pure being is actually nothing. Being and nothing are therefore intertwined. This linkage Hegel calls becoming. For Sartre, being is logically prior to nothingness. Nothingness haunts being, but being is in no way dependent upon it. My view is somewhat different from the two. By observing the flow of thinking, I see its dynamism. In this dynamism, I note recurrent forms or essences. I see thinking as a kind of kaleidoscope in which conglomerates of forms or essences recur. The flow of thinking is the same as self-consciousness. Because we are self-conscious beings, we are never one with ourselves. We are always beyond ourselves. Our thinking is always dynamic and never static. Nevertheless, this does not mean that within the flow of thinking conglomerates of essences do not recur.

We are both being and becoming. Human being is the integration of being and becoming.

But this throws us into ambiguity. Many fear ambiguity. If it cannot be pinned down, then it cannot be anything worthwhile.

Some contemporary scientists see the universe as devolving and decaying. Some philosophers and theologians see the universe as evolving and progressing. Could it be both? Could thinking be both? Thinking is both a raveling and an unraveling.

The fact we have progressed technologically often blurs what thinking is. We can see more things more clearly now. Microscopes can show us objects that were once invisible to us. Telescopes can show stars and worlds even beyond the flickers of light we see in the sky. With CAT scanners and electroencephalographs, we detect processes in our bodies heretofore concealed. Ultrasounds show us our children before we can hold them in our arms. We are led to believe that such clarity clarifies thinking. But we are dead wrong. Thinking is never as clear as a bell. No matter our technological advances, thinking will remain ambiguous, more like being in a fog than hearing a clear bell. This is because of the processional nature of our thinking. Everything is in the making. Thinking points in all directions. Inevitably, thinking tries to universalize or absolutize itself via reductionism or holism. This is the nature of thinking and to deny it would be to deny thinking itself.

Our common perceptions show us a universe in change. The sciences have validated our common perceptions. Philosophies of education talk about change, but often in the superficial way. This understanding of change concerns empirical change and not change as it relates to thinking. Though perhaps the world is accepted in all its permutations and dynamism, thinking remains fixed and rigid. The dynamism of thinking has not been well rendered in philosophies of education, even the works of the greats of the twentieth century: Whitehead, Dewey, and Freire. As much as I respect these giants, I believe they do not pinpoint the essence of thinking. About the only philosophers who have even come close to capturing the essence of thinking are Hegel and Sartre.

Thinking can be religious or philosophical. It is religious when it is static and unregenerative. For religious thinkers, first principles are treated as icons. For philosophical thinkers, thinking is processional. Regenerative thinking is the process of developing and redeveloping the world. Regenerative thinking is a continuum in which our world-views are constantly being recycled. Regenerative thinking runs roughshod over icons.

Assume all human encounters are teaching-learning and learning-teaching. The teaching-learning experience can be either religious or philosophical. If religious, then nobody thinks outside the box. Do the religious even know they are inside a box? Philosophical thinking is inimical to the status quo. Status quos perish at the hands of thinking. When we adopt the processional, we immediately make ourselves into pariahs and nomads. Pariahs and nomads because thinking sets us apart from religious cults. Regenerative thinking breaks bounds. It is always out of bounds. It is always irreverent. If teachers really mean what they always say ("I teach my students to think"), then revolution would occur instantly. Once people realize that thinking is not vague abstraction, but an intrinsic interconnectedness with their world, then they believe that things can be changed. The false dichotomy between thinking and doing is thereby extinguished. Thinking is doing and doing is thinking.

It's either religion or philosophy. It all comes down to that choice. Either we want to preserve our icons (our hallowed traditions) or change them. For those who cry for "reform," I cry "Ku Klux Klan member without sheets." They want the same system, only in a different shape. Reform means nothing more than the same ground chuck being used, but this time instead of calling it hamburger, we throw some tomato sauce on it, add some chopped onions, and call it meat loaf.

It's either philosophy or religion. If it's philosophy, then welcome to the playground of ambiguity. Truths are needles in the haystack, but that is complicated by asking: which haystack? I suggest that where being and becoming meet, we find truth. This is the right haystack. Examining the nature of our thinking is the right haystack.

Thinking is characterized by belief fading into doubt and doubt fading into belief. We can never eradicate doubt. We can never eradicate belief.

All thinking consists of interconnectedness. We are naturally beings who connect one thing with another. This is part of our natural curiosity. To those who say that curiosity killed the cat, I reply: "It may have killed the cat, but it also enriched the cat's life before the cat's unfortunate demise." To know what anything is is to understand the interconnectedness of that thing with other things. In understanding anything, we cannot isolate it as if it had the plague, or worse, bad breath. But this is the objective of compartmentalization.

Die soon, Compartmentalization.

We cannot understand anything by ignoring or being indifferent to its interconnectedness. Its being is in its interconnectedness. This is not to take the popular view that emphasizes "difference" over everything else. A view that only emphasizes difference emphasizes the alien nature of the related whole. Nothing is without contrast. Things must "stand out" if they exist at all for us. They stand out in contrast. But such contrasts or differences are not the end of the story. Things exist in their interconnectedness with other things. The more deeply we look at anything, the more we notice it has many more relationships with other things than we first imagined. The relationships between things are the basis for the understanding of a thing. This is why I say that interconnectedness is the essence of all thinking.

Our knowledge is never of any particular objects, but between objects. In other words, we know V by W, X, Y, and Z. The truth lies not within objects, but between them and in the integration of being and becoming.

Interconnectedness is essential to understanding. When philosophers say, for instance, that universals are relations, they are saying something along the same lines I am saying. The more we recognize interconnections, the fuller our understanding of an object, but also the emptier our understanding. The more interconnections we discover, the more profound our understanding. But the more profound our understanding, the more ambiguous it is.

Profundity has an essential relationship with ambiguity. I reject the Cartesian notion that we know when things are clear and distinct. Clearness and distinctness belong only to the first trimester of inquiry. Something is clear and distinct only because only a few interconnections have been discovered. Clearness and distinctness represents a shallow perspective on anything. As our knowledge of anything deepens, it becomes at the same time clear and distinct and ambiguous and indistinct. Our knowledge is a becoming-being recognizing ever-more interconnections. Compartmentalized schooling prevents knowledge from emerging. We grasp nothing in isolation. I grasp only in relation. I grasp interconnectedness. The grandest sense of interconnectedness and integration is reserved for metaphysics.

Such views have interesting ramifications for pedagogy. "Truths" do not reside in individuals. "Truths" reside between persons, in dialogue. People are interpreters of the world, but interpretation has a nuance of meaning hidden to many. "Interpret" is derived from the Latin "*interpres,*" which means "negotiator" or "explainer." When we interpret, we are in a sense negotiating between different perspectives, attempting to reconcile some with others. We negotiate between varied perspectives.

The most profound negotiation we call "philosophy." The least profound negotiation we call "religion." Religion never bargains. It simply ordains and asserts. It is a monopoly that does not need to bargain. Philosophy always bargains. And it bargains in good faith. Philosophers come to the bargaining table attempting to reconcile the grievances of different parties. The focus of philosophy is on interconnections. Philosophical negotiation never ceases, for ever more and deeper interconnections are discovered. Critical thinking is the art of negotiation. Of our philosophers, the best are the best negotiators. As we know, religion does not want to negotiate. Religion demands. Religion allows for no give and take. Philosophy is give and take. Giving and taking is how truth emerges. Such giving and taking is the essence of dynamic interconnectedness or integration.

Philosophy is negotiation.

Negotiation is "between" differences. Negotiation leads to discovering interconnectedness. I find myself not in myself and not in others, but between myself and others. Being is interconnectedness. We are rooted only because of interconnectedness. Our dynamism is the ceaseless negotiation between varied perspectives. This represents our uprootedness.

I am trying to establish a philosophy of education that commences with a new understanding of being and becoming. We are rooted in interconnectedness on every level. This is our being. Concomitant with our rootedness is our uprootedness. These are our ceaseless interpretations or negotiations between ourselves and others. Our dynamism or uprootedness is never indifference to others or in isolation from them. It is readjustment or reformulation. Readjustment and reformulation of perspectives are what we call "negotiation." The give and take of negotiation suggests interconnectedness. The art of negotiation is the art of interconnectedness.

This book discusses becoming-being in light of four thinkers: Nietzsche, Whitehead, Dewey, and Freire. I attempt to formulate my own pedagogy of dynamism by negotiating with these thinkers as well as others.

Nietzsche's inversion of Platonism goes too far. Nietzsche realizes that facing becoming without creativity is the same as sending soldiers to war without weapons. This is a key point. But Nietzsche misses the mark on becoming insofar as his inquiry focuses only on becoming in the empirical sense.

Dewey is one of the most renowned thinkers of the United States. Yet his philosophy of education, because it is rooted in empiricism, is shallow. This prevents him from offering any important description of thinking. He comes no closer to depicting thinking than a cave person approaches nuclear energy by rubbing together two rocks. Stupidly clear things are what we need to avoid at all costs. To hold tight to a shallow and contrived cohesiveness, order, and systematization is to avoid thinking. Because thinking is relational, it tends to become blurry and ambiguous. As Conrad P. Pritscher and I point out in our *In Praise of Pariahs and Nomads,*[3] chaos is the ground for thinking. I am appalled by what passes as order. Dewey describes a shallow order, systematization, and cohesiveness. Genuine thinking looks for a deeper order. Genuine thinking embraces contradictions, paradoxes, and lacunae.

Whitehead is right to say that schooling must rid itself of inert ideas. But ideas will always remain inert unless dialogue supplants lecture and the teacher-student and teaching-learning dichotomies are eliminated. I, too, want dynamic rather than inert ideas. But I recognize that radicalism, not reform, is the way to dynamize the classroom..

Deeper order is not a pat dialectical order, a Hegelian teleological scheme. Deeper order is related to the dynamic nature of thinking finding the truth between itself and others. Thinking always produces a strange residue. Thinking is never $49 \div 7 = 7$, but $49 \div 8 = 6$ with a remainder. There is always a remainder in thinking.

The mania for banal systematization manifests anal retentiveness. Anal retentiveness tries to push us off the continuum of thinking. But it never succeeds in pushing us away from the continuum.

Thinking regenerates itself. This is the source of rootedness in thinking. Interconnections are continually regenerated. All thinking, even shallow thinking, rests on interconnections.

Basing a philosophy of education on becoming-being means rejecting conservatism and traditionalism. It also means that we lead students to address what Paulo Freire calls "fear of freedom." Fear of freedom focuses on the ambiguity that arises from the rupture of platitude, tradition, and familiarity. For Freire, fear of freedom concerns how the oppressed react as they attempt to break the chains of the oppressors. For me, the fear of freedom concerns the ambiguity inherent in thinking. Fear of freedom consists of fear of ambiguity, process, and doubt.

Freire dismisses sectarianism of both the right and left for predetermining the future and eliminating freedom. We cannot be free unless we are capable of determining the future ourselves. Believing that the future is inevitable prevents us from realizing our freedom. Leftist sectarianism views the communist utopia as imminent. Rightist sectarianism wants to transplant the present custom, inherited from the past, into the future. In a radical pedagogy, people view the future as open and is not viewed in a fatalistic sense.

Creativity goes hand-in-hand with a philosophy of becoming. Meaning is not something that can be picked up, like a loaf of bread, at a convenience store. Meaning is something that human beings create through their actions.

Freedom goes hand-in-hand with a philosophy of dynamism. Freedom to create is possible only if spaces for thinking are created. Thinking does not simply point to possibilities, but is possibilities.

The project of education, the whole human project, is aimed toward the increasing humanization of human beings. This is the Good. Dehumanization is the corresponding evil. Freire's pedagogy is rooted in that value judgment.

Nietzsche understands human beings as valuers. We attach value to things, even before we measure and deliberate on them. All facts are facts qua values. There is no such thing as pure information, if we mean by this term something divorced from fact. Questions of value are inherently questions of ethics. And questions of ethics are inherently political questions, since ethical actions take place within a political framework.

For Freire, critical thinking means critical action. For him, an indivisible solidarity exists between people and the world. In the first place, in naming the world, we are acting on it. Naming is action. Secondly, divorcing thinking from acting can be seen as an ideological tool of the oppressors, who want the oppressed to believe that theory (abstract, not applicable to the world) and the world are irreconcilable. Thirdly, viewing theory and practice as wed encourages experimentation and is conducive to dynamism. Thinking is most dynamic when it tests possibilities in the world and thus invents more possibilities.

Dewey is a good empiricist.

This is his downfall.

Whatever is beyond the sense organs and scientific method should be discarded. For Dewey, the notion of a reality behind the subject is to be roundly rejected.[4] Dewey wants to bring philosophy down to earth. He abhors all forms of absolutism because absolutes are isolated and thus cannot be judged. Unfortunately, in bringing philosophy down to earth, Dewey ignores the beyond or transcendence inherent in all acts of thinking. In eliminating the beyond of traditional theology and metaphysics, Dewey eliminates the beyond inherent in all thinking. The very make-up of our self-consciousness always points us in the direction of the beyond. Philosophy of education must begin, to reiterate, with a discussion of the nature of human beings. And that brings us back to thinking. We cannot hope to understand any philosophy of dynamism, much less a pedagogy of dynamism, without first beginning with the nature of our thinking.

Dewey realizes that philosophy absorbed only with the "beyond" cannot relate to the practical affairs of human beings. He is right to demand of philosophy "a human means for determining judgments as to what is good and evil" instead of leaving these matters to supernatural means.[5]

Instead of doing a surgical bombing, however, Dewey completely annihilates the transcending nature of our being. This amounts to a fatal error. We must remember that Dewey, along with his empiricist counterparts, are in reaction to Hegel and Hegelianism. Their answer to Hegel obscures human reality. Hegel probably knows this reality better than probably anybody. For Hegel understands the dynamism of thinking. He realizes that becoming and being are wed. He also realizes that the power of negativity as the dynamism of thinking.

Freire's fear of freedom actually consists of fear of chaos, confusion, process, doubt, and ambiguity. Fear of ambiguity is actually fear of thinking. Fear of thinking, that is the problem. Contemporary pedagogy strives for "clear thinking," which it equates with critical thinking. Frequently, clear thinking is nothing more than shallow thinking. Ambiguity is driven out of such thinking, in the same way that people with AIDS are sometimes shunned. Clear thinking is simply a myth. Thinking is both light and dark. Thinking does not become progressively clearer, so that one day everything will look like a windshield after a car wash. Smudges always appear in thinking. Black holes always appear in thinking. Artificially attempting to eliminate smudges and black holes is the aim of today's critical thinking.

In thinking light and darkness intertwine. We must not forget this or else our attempts to cultivate thinking will be in vain.

The title of my book (another great title, I must say) is: *Negotiating Toward Truth: The Extinction of Teachers and Students*. My oldest daughter, Laura (of

Lauramachean Ethics fame), inquired about the "Extinction of Teachers and Students" part of the title. She wanted to know: "Do you mean that bad teachers and bad students are going to become extinct, and that only the good teachers (like you, Dad) and the good students (like me, Dad) will be left? Or do you mean that all teachers and all students will become extinct?"

I wish for the day of the extinction of all teachers and all students. This means the disassembling of all hierarchy in the classroom. That will only be possible if hierarchy everywhere in the society is eliminated. Within an authoritarian, dehumanized, and oppressive society, nonauthoritarian, humanized, and nonoppressive schooling cannot occur except by some sort of freak of nature. I am that freak.

The first part of the book's title clarifies the last part. The truth is something that must be negotiated. In order to grasp the meaning of something, we must know its interconnections. To grasp those interconnections, we must negotiate between differing perspectives. Negotiating occurs via dialoguing. Without negotiation, we cannot hope to cultivate a holistic vision of the world. Negotiating in good faith implies an awareness and reconciliation of differing perspectives. Such negotiations are creative acts and all creative acts are dynamic. Negotiation is not a hodgepodge of perspectives, or a mosaic. Thus I am not advocating eclecticism of any sort. Insight must pull these perspectives together. Insight arises in negotiation, in the integration of being and becoming or dynamism.

I am a firm advocate of what I call "intellectual promiscuity." The more intellectual promiscuity, the better. Intellectual promiscuity implies constant negotiation and integration with other perspectives. Intellectual promiscuity implies an insatiable desire to deepen knowledge and wisdom. This desire can only be fulfilled in our meetings with others, not in the form of domination but in the form of love, as negotiators intent on integration.

We must throw the baby out with the bath water because the educational system has failed in any significant way (1) to cultivate risktaking, experimentation, and innovation; (2) to embrace real dialogue (authentic moments, moments of dissent and difference); (3) to capture the dynamism of thinking; (4) to model democracy; (5) to cultivate wisdom; (6) to expose hidden and evident hierarchies; (7) to espouse intellectual promiscuity; (8) to escape paternalism; (9) to adopt a deep holistic attitude; (10) to see education as transformative, not only individually but collectively; (11) to recognize that common ground cannot be built upon inauthentic interaction but upon true dialogue and moments of difference; and (12) to liberate. As a means to maintain the status quo, the educational system must never truly address or rectify any of the failings mentioned above. The educational system can never be more than a beast in the bath water. As a means to maintain the status quo, it can never be anything else.

ONE

NIETZSCHE'S TREATMENT OF BECOMING: NARROWING IS BROADENING HORIZONS

Unlike Dewey, Whitehead, and Freire, Nietzsche does not come to mind as a philosopher of education. Like the other three, Nietzsche affirms becoming in the human experience. Nietzsche's affirmation of becoming is resounding, as the doctrines of the eternal recurrence of the same and *amor fati* suggest. His fundamental teaching is this: embrace and love becoming instead of recoiling from and loathing it. I turn to Nietzsche because his treatment of becoming offers many valuable clues for constructing a pedagogy that affirms dynamism.

1. Forgetting and Becoming

As much as Nietzsche affirms becoming, he is acutely aware of its harmful effects. This is evident in his early work, *On the Uses and Disadvantages of History for Life.*[1] Without the power to forget, Nietzsche argues, we cannot cope. Swept up into and lost in the stream of becoming, we are rendered inert. We cannot act. Action demands forgetting, a narrowing of the horizon of choices. Individuals and societies perish because of their inability to forget. The unhistorical and the historical are equally necessary for human beings. Forgetting and remembering are equally important. The trick is to learn when to remember and when to forget. We flourish to the extent we master this trick.

Nietzsche believes that in his age the doctrines of becoming have become sovereign. Characteristic of his age is "the fluidity of all concepts, types and kinds."[2] The result of the fluidity of concepts is petteness, misery, ossification, and selfishness. Instead of creating in the midst of fluidity, we become rigid in our behavior. We follow inert traditions or fail to break free from habitual forms of behavior. Affirmation of becoming demands more than acknowledging that the world is constantly changing. It demands a pro-active stance of creating change.

Nietzsche extols creativity and the value creator. The *Übermensch* is the ultimate value creator, transvaluing Judeo-Christian values. The *Übermensch* is like the child in famous "Three Metamorphoses" of *Zarathustra,* whose creative acts forge new beginnings.[3] These new beginnings are "forgettings" of the past. Creativity functions not only as an antidote to ossification, but also as preventative medicine for inertia.

We must enclose ourselves in a limited horizon if we are going to flourish. Thus, being unhistorical is essential to become a flourishing being. But Nietzsche calls on us to become superhistorical as well. By this, he means to turn away from becoming and to utilize the eternalizing powers of art and religion. Science is inimical to us insofar as it focuses only on the empirical and thus discloses pure change.

From the preceding discussion, I draw the following conclusion: Mere acknowledgment of becoming is not enough to guarantee the affirmation of becoming. When Nietzsche refers to the eternalizing forces of art and religion, he is broadly speaking of the powers of human creativity. The affirmation of becoming is not possible without the power of creativity. This points to the vital interconnection between creativity and the affirmation of becoming.

A pedagogy of dynamism must also be a pedagogy of creativity. Sending students to becoming without having cultivated their creativity is like sending warriors to battle without weapons. The outcome is obvious. Becoming can be affirmed only when we are able to transform the world. What exactly does that mean? We can put our image on the world. At the end of *On the Advantage and Disadvantage of History for Life,* Nietzsche maintains that the ancient Greeks, his paradigm of a healthy, world-affirming people, flourished because they were able to organize the chaos by reflecting on their genuine needs and by allowing sham needs to perish.[4] This is a lesson we must all learn, says Nietzsche.

Being swept up into becoming means not having any control of our world. The fluidity becomes ours when we invest it with our image. Creativity is requisite for investing the world with our image. Creative acts limit the world and infinite possibilities. In limiting the world, we create what Pierre Furter calls "scope."[4]

Without creativity, we are passive beings at the mercy of becoming. We then retreat into the security of our traditions and habits. In order to insure our flourishing, the dynamism of becoming must be molded through creative acts. Fear of becoming is overcome only insofar as creativity is accentuated in schooling.

The creative have no fear of becoming. It can be molded and shaped. For those reared in Freire's banking concept of education, becoming or dynamism is a danger. Their response to becoming, as Nietzsche points out, is ossification. Ossification correlates closely to Freire's "fear of freedom."[5] The oppressed seek security rather than liberty. They prefer ossification, following the precepts set up by the oppressors, because they refuse to take the responsibility for creating their own beliefs. They prefer rigidity because of their perceived inability to create.

Nietzsche excoriates Occidental philosophers for denying that the world is essentially becoming. Western philosophy is criticized for opposing being to becoming and for valuing the static over the dynamic. In *The Will to Power,* Nietzsche makes a curious statement seemingly contradicting his adversarial stance regarding the static: "To impose upon becoming the character of being—that is the supreme will to power."[6] Nietzsche does not contradict himself by affirming being over becoming. To impose being on becoming is to be able to create out of becoming. It means to impose our vision on the world. For Nietzsche, this represents the supreme act.

Imposing being on becoming is the supreme act of self-determination. The world becomes ours by shaping and organizing becoming. The complex of beliefs that swirl before us and confuse us can be categorized by the creative mind into a coherent world.

I have just described fear of becoming. Fear of becoming is closely related to hatred of becoming. In *Twilight of the Idols,* Nietzsche condemns Occidental philosophers for their hatred of becoming.[7] Death, change, old age, procreation, and growth contradict what they believe is true: an Unchanging Reality. From the perspective of the mainstream of western philosophers, anything the senses show us is a lie. For Nietzsche, not the senses but what we make out of the senses is a lie. Whenever we abstract, we introduce metaphysical lies into the world. On the other hand, the testimony of the senses reveals to us the world as it actually is. Metaphysical abstractions like unity, thinghood, substance, and permanence are the lies. Our immediate sense experience represents the truth.

We fear what we hate and hate what we fear. We mistrust whatever we hate and fear. For Nietzsche, the ultimate fear of human beings is becoming. Nietzsche's doctrines of the eternal recurrence of the same and *amor fati* are the ultimate affirmation of becoming. The doctrines of the eternal recurrence of the same and *amor fati* entails that we love life for what it is: the pain, the suffering, the joy, the humiliation, the sorrow, everything. It also means we wouldn't want our lives altered in any way to avoid life. We neither fear nor hate life. We trust, love, and embrace life.

Fear of becoming is closely related to fear of creativity. Becoming points in an infinite number of directions and thus presents an infinite number of possibilities. In limiting possibilities, creative acts make people aware of their responsibility in creating the world. But as existentialists like Sartre have suggested, people often "flee" from the responsibility of ownership of their acts. This "fleeing" from ownership is actually fear of taking responsibility for creating our world. Thus I fear becoming because it points back to me, making me the creative agent, the author, of meaning in my life.

Hatred of becoming is closely linked with suffering. Healthy, well-adjusted human beings can affirm the world of becoming. This is because they possess the creative powers to unify the world without denying it. Sufferers cannot affirm the world of becoming. They must replace it with a world of being, of changelessness. This is their solace. They conceive of a world in which contradiction is absent. This represents a creative act, but one born out of suffering, not overflowing health.

Occidental philosophers suffer from what Nietzsche calls *ressentiment*. An English word resembling the French word *ressentiment is* resentment. But resentment does not capture the special meaning that Nietzsche confers to *ressentiment. Ressentiment* is a form of hatred especially experienced by the oppressed. Their bottled up hatred for their oppressors becomes creative. They take the values of the oppressors and invert them. Their oppressors value, for example, aggressiveness and devalue meekness. The oppressed invert the values such that meekness becomes a value; aggressiveness, a disvalue.

What Nietzsche means can be made clearer by remembering the Aesop fable of the fox and the grapes. The fox desires to possess the delicious grapes, greatly valuing them. But the grapes are up too high in the tree for the fox to reach. Repeated attempts by the fox to reach the grapes fail. The fox then comes to believe that the grapes are sour. The fox inverts the value of the grapes, believing they are sour, not sweet. This alleviates a tension between desiring something and not being able to attain it.

We do not know whether the fox experiences a temporary or permanent inversion of values. *Ressentiment* is a permanent inversion of values. It alleviates suffering by easing the tension between desiring something and not being able to attain it.

In general, western thinkers have been oppressed by the world of becoming. It makes them suffer. They are people who want to live, but cannot. They cannot affirm the world of becoming, so they negate it. They create a world of being in which contradictions cease to exist. This, too, is a creative act, but one arising from suffering, *ressentiment.*

If creativity arises from hatred of becoming, then we can create abstractions that deny becoming and create a false world of being. In the positive sense, creative acts are transformative and thus affirm change. Our faith in ourselves to shape and mold the world arises from such affirmation of change.

Sufferers cannot stand in the face of contradiction. Their minds cannot be boggled because of an implicit fear that the mind cannot be unboggled. The mind that is not boggled is the mind that never thinks. When contradictions arise, then we experience a tension between the desire to know and our inability to do so. But this is what we must bear in order to know.

We talk about possessing knowledge. We supposedly possess knowledge, in the way we own cars, videos, and homes. We desire knowledge in the same way the fox wants the grapes. When many persons cannot possess "knowledge" and solve problems with clear-cut solutions, then they negate this knowledge. It isn't worth seeking anyway, they say. This is why many people cannot stand philosophy. But their hatred of philosophy is tantamount to the hatred of becoming, contradiction, and life.

Nietzsche's characterization of *ressentiment* lacks an appreciation (as might be expected from him) for the oppressed. The oppressed are unable to affirm becoming because they are, as Freire says, ambiguous beings.[8] They have a dual identity. They are beings who seek to discover their own identities, but house the image of the oppressor (internalization of the image of the oppressor). They are crippled from imposing "being" on the world because of the conflict within.

Nietzsche notes the different physiologies and psychologies behind the same value. Values can be the product of vitality and the affirmation of life or degeneration and the negation of life. Vital, world-affirming human beings can withstand a Dionysian perspective on reality. Dionysians can affirm the suffering and pain of life and becoming. Those who suffer from an impoverishment of life want their art and knowledge to have a soothing, palliative effect.

The rationale for destruction may arise from an overfullness or an impoverishment of life. Dionysians embrace destruction because from destruction issues a new birth. Dionysians welcome destruction because destruction is part of the creative process. They have faith in the future because they believe they can be architects of it. On the other hand, destructiveness can arise from people who hate life.[9]

Creativity is not always in the service of life and may be a profound disservice to it. Only when creativity affirms becoming is it condoned by Nietzsche. Nietzsche urges us to evaluate the psychology and the physiology behind evaluations of becoming. The healthiest human beings are those who regenerate themselves and their knowledge. They possess the creativity necessary to recreate their worlds.

From my perspective, dialogue is the best means for demonstrating the dynamism of ideas in the classroom. But as important as the dynamism of ideas is their regeneration. A pedagogy of dynamism takes place within the framework of a recurrent conglomeration of essences. Without both aspects, thinking cannot occur. As Conrad P. Pritscher and I conclude in *Pariahs and Nomads, arche* and anarchy are tied together.[10] Creativity can generate new beginnings, fresh insights and beliefs. Persons without the faith in their powers of regeneration will not be able to face becoming. Faith in the power of creativity is the most important thing that will ever be cultivated in a person. The creative can change themselves and the world. Becoming does not ossify them, but stimulates them to regenerate the recurrent conglomeration of essences in unique ways.

2. Purpose and Becoming

Our discussion shifts from forgetting and becoming to purpose and becoming. Fear, hatred, and revenge are the principal enemies of a pedagogy of dynamism.

They prevent us from affirming becoming at the very least, and negating it in the most extreme case.

According to Nietzsche, when we refer to becoming, we do not want to fall into the mistake of believing that the universe is moving toward a goal. Becoming has no goal. The universe is not moving toward the Last Judgment or Hegel's Absolute Knowing. Related to this, people cannot take refuge in the thought of being part of grand unity. This suggests being part of a master plan, as for example, the thesis of the "best of all possible worlds," which asserts that no matter what happens, it is always part of God's grand scheme of things.

In contrast, Nietzsche conceives becoming as a great ring. A ring has no beginning or end.[11] Nietzsche's eternal recurrence of the same affirms the circularity of becoming. If we affirm one part of the ring of becoming, then we affirm every other part of it. One point is the same as all the others. Each point leads nowhere in the sense that nowhere is contrasted with an ultimate goal.

Human beings do not play designated roles in a universal melodrama. We must create our own goals. We introduce purpose into the universe. Whether the universe possesses an ultimate purpose or a grand unity is beyond the purview of human knowledge. But evidently, we can create purpose for ourselves. These purposes are the vision that we impose on becoming. This is our being, to impose a vision on the world. Our being is our creativity.

For Nietzsche, abstraction is the source of lies. Our senses show us a world full of contradictions and that for Nietzsche is what the world really is. When we logicalize the world and introduce categories, we make it more calculable for ourselves. Categories do not reveal the truth to us, but help us gain security and offer us an abbreviated way to comprehend the world. Concepts like substance, object, being, and becoming are not metaphysical truths, but serve our needs. Accordingly, when we examine equality and similarity, we see that both represent a way to shape something to fit into an already existing scheme of things. Nietzsche likens this to the assimilation of inorganic matter. Equality does not have a metaphysical status, for example, Plato's ειδοσ of equality. Equality, like other concepts, serves our needs, just as changing colors serves the needs of a chameleon.

Systematized philosophy for Nietzsche is a lie. It gives the impression that contradictions can be ironed out and contributes to ascribing categories to the universe. This leads in the direction of positing a grand scheme or purpose to the universe.

Systematization or a movement toward order or coherence cannot be avoided. No matter that Nietzsche frequently writes aphoristically and cryptically and avoids systematization in the fashion of a Kant or a Hegel—this does not mean an absence of a system. Concepts like the will to power, eternal recurrence of the same, *amor fati*, the *Übermensch*, the Dionysian and Apollonian, and *ressentiment* cohere. On the other hand, Nietzsche does not really advocate irrationalism. He takes the position that human beings flourish when reason is in the service of our instincts. A distinction between generalizations and abstractions may be of some use here. Generalizations are a necessary facet of imposing our vision on the world. Drawing inferences and making interconnections entails generalizations. Nietzsche, I believe, would have no problem with generalizations. His problem would be with abstractions, when these generalizations become metaphysical concepts that point toward a transcendent and unchanging reality.

In the Nietzschean universe, we are free to create. The future is not set, but is open to our vision. Nietzsche's vision for humanity is the *Übermensch*. In a pedagogy of dynamism, students must be encouraged to bring about their own visions of the world. They must never be suffocated by a sense of fatalism. This sense of fatalism can be cosmic or institutional. Institutional fatalism is the belief that we can to do nothing to alter our present political and social conditions. Cosmic fatalism is the belief that no matter what we do, we are part of a larger cosmic plan over which we have no control.

What is the relationship between these two forms of fatalism? I contend they have a bearing on one another. Belief in the dynamism of reality, that we can initiate change, dissolves institutional fatalism. If we cannot initiate change, then we fall back onto cosmic fatalism as a means of security. Instead of securing ourselves via our creativity, cosmic fatalism roots us. But creativity can counteract such pseudo-rootedness. Only creativity can prevent us from falling into institutional and cosmic fatalism.

If becoming has no goal, then shouldn't we become distraught, give up and commit suicide? This is the sentiment of the person who is disconcerted upon realizing the aimlessness of the universe. A sense of nihilism arises when we lose the center of our beliefs. We become uncentered and uprooted. When we are robbed of our creativity, then we become nihilistic. I suggest that if we lead creative lives, nihilism is bound to dissolve. Nihilism is not fundamentally the response to a universe without purpose, but is the response of a person and society without purpose. If the shackles of oppressions are shorn, nihilism dissolves. The more empowered people are, the more creative, then the less nihilistic. The more disenfranchised, the more nihilistic. The more unable to control the social and political world, the more nihilistic.

Cosmological nihilism is the outgrowth of institutional or political nihilism. Remove political nihilism and you remove the other form of nihilism. A pedagogy of dynamism must never allow nihilism to emerge. Nihilism is less likely to emerge when creativity is not stiffled. People who have a voice in government and are able to actualize the kind of life they believe is just and good do not become nihilists. Who really cares whether God is dead? We should be more concerned about our creativity being dead. Perhaps when our creativity is resurrected, then so will God.

3. Revaluation and Becoming

For Nietzsche, all of our sense perceptions are suffused with value, for example, the harmful (and what arises from it, the unpleasant) and the useful (and what arises from it, the pleasant). Our senses select perceptions useful to our preservation. Even the perception of color is an expression of value inasmuch as preferring this color to that is a means to preservation.[12]

At the base of Nietzsche's metaphysics is the claim that human beings are evaluative beings. Apparently, we cannot be anything but evaluative beings. We are as much evaluative as we are evolving beings. The gist of Nietzsche's message is this: Those persons (Goethe) and civilizations (the Greeks) who live according to their instincts flourish. In such cases, the instincts have not been corrupted.[13] Once the instincts have become corrupted, then we value badly. For Nietzsche, this means we value things that are life-negating. Those whose instincts have not become corrupt make life-affirming value judgments. A correlation exists between physiology and valuation. The more vital make life-affirming valuations. The less vital make life-negating valuations.

Life-negating valuations are closely connected with the denial of becoming as ultimate reality. Life-negating valuations are rooted in the assumption of a transcendent and unchanging reality. Logicalizing or categorizing can become the basis for conceiving a realm of permanence. Traditional metaphysical concepts of substance, subject, thing, causality, and being militate against the affirmation of the world of becoming. An indication of a vital human being is one who can affirm becoming as it is: an affirmation of the eternal recurrence of the same.

Human beings have had too much faith in reason, says Nietzsche. We would be more vital if reason were the handmaiden to the instincts. We are a complex of instincts expressing themselves in the form of domination. We are, as Nietzsche says, will to power. No self directs our action. I do not have a body. My body has an "I." The ego does not direct the body. Rather drives in the body direct the ego.

One of the primary themes of Nietzsche's thought is overcoming. Nietzsche praises life-affirming values that provide a means to overcoming. When a value system no longer promotes affirmation, then it must be overcome. The vital human being is able to overcome values and beliefs and to create new ones. There is a kind of innocence in creating, the innocence of a child at play.

Overcomers create their own image of the world and create their own values. No value is eternal for Nietzsche. If you leave meat out on the counter for several days, it will become rancid. It will no longer be edible. The same applies to values. They are perishables. They decay. When they decay, we must create other values to replace them. We must overcome these values; we must transvalue.

Human beings (at least some human beings, from Nietzsche's aristocratic perspective) are capable of transforming themselves and their values. Their vitality depends upon such transformation.

Our human nature is to overcome, make, and remake ourselves. Our being is becoming. The more fully we can transform ourselves, the more fully human we are. To put it in other terms, the more creative we are, the more human we can become.

Let me backtrack for a moment and reiterate some ideas concerning forgetting and becoming. Fear, hatred, and revenge are the principal enemies of becoming. These emotions block an affirmation of becoming. Do they also block an affirmation of overcoming? Yes, and this is because of the intrinsic relationship between the affirmation of becoming and overcoming. Becoming is denied or ignored by those who lack the belief in their creative faculties. Thus, such people deny or ignore overcoming.

Pedagogy must begin with an understanding of the nature of human beings. If we assume that human beings are creative, we also make the assumption of their being able to overcome obstacles.

Human being is becoming increasingly more creative. If pedagogy is for the benefit of human beings, then it must cultivate creativity. Yet we can understand why oppressors can never allow much creativity to be cultivated in schooling. Ideas would suddenly become alive for students. Students would transform themselves and their beliefs would no longer conform to the predominant ideology.

We must remember that for Nietzsche the ultimate goal is the revaluation of all values. Judeo-Christian values no longer help us affirm life. By abiding by defunct values, we harm ourselves. For him, only a few persons are capable of creating new values. The masses can only follow. Great human beings are a rarity; most are bad imitators of the few great human beings.

I reject Nietzsche's elitism. We have yet to create a society in which the majority of human beings can flourish. By flourish, I do not mean what others mean by "progress," as in technological advance. I mean the nurturing of creativity in every facet in a society. Self-determination is an empty word without removing all forms of oppression in a society. For Nietzsche, the masses are simply the means to great human beings. They are the placenta to the neonate. Since only a few can be great human beings, then it is a simple step to saying that only a few can rule a society. If we take another route and say that most human beings can be creative, then it is a simple step to saying that human beings can rule themselves.

Nietzsche sees human beings as instinctive creatures who have overly relied on their reason. This leads him to an anti-metaphysical stance in which concepts like "being" and "essence" are seen as life-negating diseases that threaten the lifeblood of the species. Nietzsche has made a profound misdiagnosis. Human beings are an integration of being and becoming, of the permanent and the dynamic. Self-consciousness is dynamism, but within this dynamism recurs certain conglomeration of essences. Creative acts determine the specific configuration of the essential conglomerations. My creative acts, for example, have conglomerated the essences of freedom, self-determination, hope, and justice. These disparate essences cohere and are dynamized in the act of creation. So long as these essences continually recreate, they cannot become sterile or life-negating. This point will be developed further in the final chapter.

Nietzsche's insights into the nature of forgetting illuminate the nature of the creative act. The creative act is both limiting and expansive. While the range of disconnected possibilities shrinks, the range of interconnected possibilities emerges. When the range of disconnected possibilities is transformed into a range of interconnected possibilities, despair is transformed into hope. We experience despair over the prospect of a myriad of unrelated possibilities. We experience hope when creative acts fuse and interconnect possibilities.

4. Democracy, Dialogue, Trust, Becoming, and Creativity

Democracy, dialogue, trust, becoming, and creation have an intrinsic relationship. I have already delineated the relationship between becoming and creation. Creativity is requisite for affirming dynamism. We can affirm becoming because we can mold and shape it. Mistrust of our creativity means mistrust of becoming. Dynamism cannot be affirmed until we are creatively prepared to meet it.

Dialogue is perhaps the best way to demonstrate dynamism. But the dynamism of the world is frightening to many persons because they lack belief in the formative power. Dialogue boggles the mind. We must be able to unboggle it.

When we mistrust creativity, we mistrust ourselves and frequently do not attribute creativity to other persons. Trusting the creativity of ourselves and of others is prerequisite for affirming democratization in all phases of our lives.

When we democratize, we trust others to create institutions that are to the benefit of other people. We trust in the creative powers of other people. We trust that most people can make decisions that benefit the whole.

For many, trust is not considered a prudent thing. Trust is seen as the enterprise of the fool. Mistrust is seen is as more prudent.

Trust in your own creativity forms the basis of a belief that nothing is beyond redemption. Nothing is unsalvageable. Whatever happens, you believe that because of your creativity, you can rectify the situation. Only if you believe in your own creativity do you believe in yourself.

For the creative, nothing is beyond redemption. When we attribute creativity to others as well to ourselves, then we believe that heaven can be brought to earth or at least closer to it.

TWO

THE INERT IDEAS OF
ALFRED NORTH WHITEHEAD

Alfred North Whitehead's Philosophy of Education?

I looked forward to reading Alfred North Whitehead's philosophy of education. Like many others, I was awed by Whitehead and Russell's *Principia Mathematica* and expected another awe-inspiring experience.

I was disappointed when I encountered the work of this supposed giant in the field. I came away half-impressed. I suppose I should not have been too disappointed. I expect shallowness from representatives of the Analytic School, even from unconventional members like Whitehead. Nothing with depth, nothing profound. For a fast food joint, Burger King is all right. For an analytic philosopher, Whitehead is all right. Ultimately, he does not capture the essence of thinking.

I have another serious problem with Whitehead as educator. You already know my position: I despise reformers. Whitehead is nothing more than a reformer. I want to use "reformer" in the most pejorative sense I can think of and cast every aspersion I can at it. Reformers often make themselves out to be great saviors, but they deceive people into believing deep changes are being made when they are not. Being a reformer means to leave the nucleus intact and to make decorative changes to the superficies. Reform is nothing more than a makeover: new hairstyle, new make-up, new clothes. But deeper changes are not made. Reform is never enough for people like myself who believe the system is evil. If you believe a system is evil, then reform is never enough. Some things are past reform. Sweat shops, concentration camps, and kiddie porn are past reform. They are abominable. So is our pitiable education system.

I don't want to spend my time reforming the reformers. I would prefer to radicalize them.

The American educational system suffocates students. When students receive their diplomas, they should not be seen as graduates, but as casualties of war. This is an intolerable situation. I resent and despise those who want to do makeovers of intolerable situations.

I am not one of those who believes that changes naturally evolve in the state of human affairs. As Martin Luther King, Jr. says in his "Letter from Birmingham City Jail," time is not neutral.[1] It can be used constructively or destructively. Great changes come about when human beings fight side-by-side, guided by a common vision.

My chief focus in this chapter is on *The Aims of Education and Other Essays*. *The Aims of Education and Other Essays* is largely (except for one chapter) a compilation of Whitehead's addresses to educational and scientific societies between 1912 and 1928. In the Preface of *The Aims of Education,* Whitehead bluntly says that the whole text "is a protest against dead knowledge, that is to say, inert ideas."[2] Something is rotten in our classrooms. It smells as if something died in there. While Whitehead's instincts are right, his attempts to expunge the blight are largely unsuccessful. To bring dynamism to ideas, dialogue is requisite. Whitehead's reformist approach merely masks the symptoms and does a disservice by suggesting that his remedy can cure the disease.

1. Inert Ideas

Whitehead pinpoints the fundamental problem in schooling: inert ideas. Ideas are mummified. Great teachers are miracle workers because they routinely resurrect inert ideas. Great teachers vivify and animate even the worst of inert ideas. Inert ideas harden the arteries of creativity and eventually form a thought blockage such that students are brain-dead. Students sit in vegetative states, and we teachers often wonder whether we should take their pulses
    In "The Aims of Education," Whitehead defines as inert ideas as "ideas that are merely received into the mind without being utilized, or tested, or thrown into fresh combinations."[3] Such "ideas" (if we wish to call them even that) are "absorbed" or memorized. Ideas become dynamized to the extent they capture our imaginations. Applying or utilizing an idea in my own life turns an inorganic into an organic idea. Unlike inorganic ideas, organic ideas can develop in my environment. Testing an idea engages me as I determine whether it is true or false. Juxtaposing ideas not normally juxtaposed often reveals surprising relationships that are the occasion for fresh insights. Ideas remain inert when they are isolated from one another or when the relationship of one idea to another is not the result of creative synthesis but of inert memorization.
    Students are rarely encouraged to develop their imaginations. Ideas are simplisticly presented to students in what I shall call the "tombstone approach." A tombstone usually has the name of the deceased, dates of birth and death, and perhaps a few words about the person. An incredibly complex person is reduced to a few simplistic facts that become his or her permanent record. Many teachers take this tombstone approach. Not only are complex subjects reduced to a few simplistic facts, but these facts are seen as static. In the classroom full of tombstones or inert ideas, everything is reduced to pedantry and routine, as Whitehead says. "Here's this tombstone and here's another. These ideas are dead and shall always remain dead."

Inert schooling is uncreative. Uncreative schooling represents the atrophy of the imagination. Without the exercise of the imagination, teachers cannot say they are creating conditions for students to do independent thinking. Nor can they say they help to develop students' autonomy. Nietzsche's "Three Metamorphoses" in *Thus Spoke Zarathustra* can help me make my point more clearly. Nietzsche believes that most people have a camel mentality whereby they bend over and shoulder the values of their society without so much as examining them.[4] Similarly, students who receive inert ideas are like camels who bend over and shoulder whatever is placed on them. "Every intellectual revolution," Whitehead writes, "which has ever stirred humanity into greatness has been a passionate protest against inert ideas."[5]

From my perspective, inert ideas can be viewed in the following ways:

(1) They can be viewed as old, tired ideas that have little significance to students.
(2) They can be deemed the result of students being passive recipients instead of imaginative integrators of ideas.
(3) They can be seen as cultivated by an inert presentation of ideas via monologue instead of via dynamic dialogue.
(4) They can be seen as disparate, compartmentalized ideas that remain stagnant in their isolation instead of interrelated ideas that become dynamic in their constant "playing off" one another.
(5) They can be viewed as arising from the traditional teacher-student hierarchy, in which some (teachers), the oracles, own knowledge, while others (students), the vessels, are to be filled with knowledge they do not own.
(6) They are fostered by aesthetic respect, a superficial respect limited to rules, regulations, titles, and the like.
(7) They are the result of isolating facts from and elevating them over values.

The seven are interrelated. Dialogue energizes ideas, even old ideas. In dialogue, students and teachers can imaginatively engage ideas. Dialogue is free-flowing and encourages creative, spontaneous integration of ideas. Facts are vivified to the extent they are located within the context of value. This is when we assess and evaluate the value of facts. Old ideas are vivified in dialogue, reconstructed and refurbished. In dialogue, ideas are "bounced off one another" such that they do not become isolated and stagnant. In dialogue, knowledge is co-created and thus co-owned rather than being the private property of teachers. Aesthetic respect, as Frantz Fanon points out, encourages compliance to existing forms of oppression and is not liberatory.[6] Respect for others suggests the recognition of them as creative and self-determining beings.

According to Whitehead, "[T]he mind is never passive; it is a perpetual activity, delicate, receptive, responsive to stimulus."[7] Eviscerating intellectual analysis and exclusively "bookish" scholastic routines make us unappreciative "of the infinite variety of vivid values in our environment."[8] These values are not the specialized values of either the practical person or scholar. These are the values of persons aesthetically attuned to their environments: "There is no substitute for the direct perception of the concrete achievement of a thing in its actuality. We want concrete fact with a high light thrown on what is relevant to its preciousness."[9] We grasp the preciousness of facts only when we have cultivated aesthetic appreciation.

The depth of individuality is linked to the development of aesthetic sensibility. Aesthetic value emerges from activity; the emergent value is a manifestation of individuality. Lacking activity or initiative, we cannot apprehend aesthetic values. Without the apprehension of aesthetic values, initiative is not possible.

Put in another way, creativity is as requisite for the apprehension of values as apprehension of values is requisite for creativity. Both spontaneity and receptivity are requisite for the emergence of values. "Sensitiveness without impulse spells decadence, and impulse without sensitiveness spells brutality."[10] Whitehead uses the term "sensitiveness" to refer to apprehending what is beyond ourselves, what he calls "all facts of the case." The word "impulse," I believe, is synonymous with creativity or initiation. Without creativity, values remain inert and abstract because they neither emerge nor are vitalized in our life activities. Without sensitiveness to value, creativity becomes a brutish act because it lacks content. Kant makes a similar point in the first *Critique* when he says that concepts without intuitions are empty and intuitions without concepts are blind.[11] Spontaneity must have content and receptivity must have form. For Whitehead, when concrete facts are arranged such that particular values emerge—this is art in the most general sense. Trying to get a good view of a lovely sunset is an instance of looking at a concrete fact (the sun) in order to see its beauty (value). Whitehead is careful to point out that aesthetic experience or art is not limited to celestial bodies or natural phenomena. The concrete fact of a factory can be viewed as art. The humming of the machinery, the patterns in which workers do their jobs, the relationship of the factory to the needs of the general population—such concrete facts can be arranged to elicit attention to vivid value and help us grasp the organism in its completeness.[12]

Abstracting ideas from life is the best way to produce inert ideas, tombstone facts. "There is only one subject-matter for education, and that is Life in all its manifestations."[13] Vital ideas arise from individual and collective life activities. These are the most pressing problems and issues of an age. The ideas of the ages become "interesting" to students inasmuch as they speak to universal concerns and interests as they are manifested in a particular society.

The insights of William James can deepen our analysis in this area. In "The Will to Believe," James distinguishes between live and dead hypotheses.[14] For technologically advanced persons of the late twentieth century, Einstein's theory of relativity is a live hypothesis. Similarly, pantheism is a dead hypothesis. This is not a question of whether something is true or not. This is a matter of believing something to be true. Expanding on James's point, I might say that an ideological framework forms the basis for live and dead hypotheses. "Blacks are lazy, shiftless, and promiscuous" was (and is still) a live hypothesis in the United States of America. Just because education focuses on live hypotheses doesn't mean that it is good. People have fed on the worst elements of human hatred and fears. Education should not simply be interesting. Interest can be cheap, base, or shallow. The ideology of the dominant class determines the parameters of live hypotheses. For instance, "progress," usually equated with technological advancement, is one of those live hypotheses. Moral and social progress are perhaps not dead ideas, but comatose ones. Students may at first resist the concept of moral and social progress because their culture has equated progress with technology. Often, live hypotheses must be cultivated.

Live hypotheses spring from particular social and political situations, but they remain narrow unless discussed within the framework of universal human themes. "The American Dream" can be viewed in terms of self-actualization, self-determination, freedom, and individualism versus collectivism. An idea becomes more vivacious the more it evokes wonder. I suggest that the most *wonderful* experience students can have is seeing how the particular fits within the whole. How do the truths of their society at that moment fit within the broader spectrum? For example, we come to realize that a similar oppressive apparatus is used in all sorts of scapegoating, whether it be Blacks, Jews, Feminists, Gays, etc. Wonder is concomitant to the imaginative, perpetually integrating mind. Ideas or hypotheses are most vital or wonderful when they integrate particulars of the person's lived experience with the recurring general patterns that characterize all thinking (God, Freedom, Immortality, the Good, the Beautiful, the Just, Oppression, Love, Evil, etc.) Vivid integration of the recurring general patterns with a person's lived experience elevates the lived experience to a universal standpoint and concretizes the universal in the lived moment. Such experiences are the zenith of education.

The experience of the wonderful is an aesthetic experience. Whitehead is right when he says that students should develop a sense of aesthetic, and that this sense of the aesthetic is a prerequisite for an appreciation of style.[15] For Whitehead, style is the attainment of an end without waste. The virtue of style is the last acquired by the educated person, a virtue acquired only after long labor. Style consists of "cultivated judgments," knowing where everything goes so that nothing is wasted. The best prose is the one that expresses the thought with the least amount of verbiage. According to this line of thought, the best classes would have little or no "wasted" time. When dialogue becomes the essence of classroom activity, then much is wasted. It isn't always the most economical.

Style comes last, but let's not forget how style is developed and redeveloped. There is often great waste involved in developing a style. It may take years of experimentation and going down wrong roads finally to grasp what our style is. The continual development of style (assuming style continually evolves) means waste. Secondly, I can point to many great philosophers whose writings undoubtedly have "style," but are hardly "economical." Kant, Hegel, Husserl.

What's wrong with a little waste or even a lot of waste? Only the shopkeeper worries about waste. And with Whitehead, we encounter the shopkeeper's values. Whitehead's thought is driven by the value of efficiency, a fundamental value of capitalism. Waste not, want not. Waste is a necessary element of creation. Assuming that we don't know what we are going to create, we will try all kinds of combinations (which Whitehead urges us to do) until what we believe is our creation emerges. If that isn't wasteful, nothing is. In a fast-paced technological society, clarity matters because we simply don't have time to explore any of the ambiguities of phenomena. Because we must quickly predict outcomes, we have little time for ambiguities, which are viewed as wasteful sidetracking.

But the exploration of ambiguities is an important element of thinking. Thus we encounter a fundamental contradiction in Whitehead. He extols the imagination, but wants to economize. Imagination wastes and wastes. It cannot be economized. I am disgusted by how the classroom has imitated the work place: controlled discourse not meant to offend but unable to enlighten; teacher evaluation forms like the kind you receive at grocery stores or car dealerships; quantitative grading as the measure of a student's success; an underlying message of accommodation, of prudent, indifferent inaction, rather than loving and revolutionary involvement.

I mistrust all thinking that gives the impression of being perfectly lucid and taut. Many notions, important to us as human beings, are beyond the pale of clarity. They are intrinsically unclear because they are on the edge of human understanding. That does not make them unimportant. In *Education and Values: In Praise of Pariahs and Nomads,* Conrad P. Pritscher and I claim that without the chaotic moment, thinking is not possible.[16] Thinking is not simply the movement from ambiguity to clarity, but from clarity to ambiguity. In other words, it is a double movement. Clarification is an element of thinking, but equally important is the movement back toward ambiguity, toward chaos. Thinking is a tension between pulling together and pushing apart. It rests on that tension. We never finish thinking because of this dynamic double movement. I see thinking at once as progression and retrogression. Thinking is hard to guide and control (untoward) and tractable (toward). Thinking is an evolving core of conglomerated ideas that attract and repel other ideas and even expel ideas from the core.

2. Freedom and Discipline

In "The Rhythmic Claims of Freedom and Discipline," Whitehead observes: "The fading of ideals is sad evidence of the defeat of the human endeavor."[17] When ideals are identical to practice, then stagnation results. Progress cannot be attained by conceiving education as the acquisition "of mechanical mental aptitudes, and of formulated statements of useful truths."[18]

Whitehead does not go far or deep enough. In the United States of America, we don't want our way of life (sexism, racism, homophobia, classism, imperialism) changed, so our education system produces narrow-minded people who rubber-stamp whatever the powers that be place in front of them. Our schooling is designed to deaden the senses and imagination and stupefy us so that we can become cogs in the wheel without much protest. Whatever is not practical, whatever does not help us gain employment, is deemed useless, archaic, inoperable.

Wherever the imagination is allowed to roam freely, hope is never far behind. Wherever the imagination is incarcerated, hope lags far behind, often so far behind that it is sometimes invisible. Ideals are real for us (not inert) only when we believe, we hope, can we bring them into being. Schooling that incarcerates the imagination incarcerates hope and ideals.

The metaphysics of empiricism also plays a role in the death of ideals. Ideals are universals. They are ultimates. A mind trained only to look at discrete facts and to analyze them can never conceive of ideals. From the perspective of empiricism, instead of being a spur to action, ideals are conceived as far-fetched delusions of the inane or the insane. Ideals cannot come into being without an imagination that is permitted to universalize and discover ultimates. Empiricism represses universalization just by the very nature of its insistence that only particulars exist.

But an abstract universalism that does not integrate and is not vitalized by lived activities is as deadly as fragmentary empiricism. Abstract universalism does not vitally integrate ideals. Ideals are as distant and as unattainable as the stars. Integration of universals with lived activities vitalizes and revitalizes ideals. Ideals no longer are seen as distant and disparate stars, but as a network of nearby and empowering power sources.

The relationship of knowledge and wisdom is central to Whitehead's philosophy of education. For Whitehead, wisdom is more important than knowledge. but wisdom without knowledge is not wisdom. Dr. Pangloss of Voltaire's *Candide* represents the intellectual whose maxims are out of touch with reality. The manner in which we hold knowledge Whitehead calls "wisdom."[19] Perhaps by this he means judgment, but then to have knowledge means to judge, too. I wish to call the judgment of knowledge compartmentalized, whereas the judgment of wisdom is holistic. By compartmentalization, I mean inert facts not vitalized by life activities that appear indifferent to and disconnected from one another by virtue of a anti-dialogical approach. Compartmentalized thinking never runs into difference. By holism, I mean dynamic facts vitalized by life activities, networked by virtue of creativity and dialogue. The more thinking runs into "boundaries," the more it meets difference. This running into "differences" I call holistic or integrative thinking. So-called wisdom spouted at us from so-called sages is not wisdom, claims Whitehead. The prerequisite for wisdom, Whitehead says, is "freedom in the presence of knowledge."[20] What is this freedom? This freedom, in its most basic sense, is the unboundedness of the imagination, which is the fulcrum of the active, creative, and spontaneous person. Whitehead, I believe, is affirming the imagination, and creativity and this represents his notion of freedom: "The habit of active thought, with freshness, can only be generated by adequate freedom."[21]

Encyclopedic knowledge does not impress Whitehead. Knowledge receives value depending on the person who possesses the knowledge and what that person does with it. Knowledge must be reorganized and recreated by the active, spontaneous, and creative mind. It must be evaluated. But more than that, and Whitehead does not say this, the value of different types of knowledge must be judged. In the Editorial Foreword to Lansana Keita's *The Human Project and the Temptations of Science*, I question whether the reductionistic truths of physics be considered first-order knowledge when they are only tangentially valuable to us as human beings.[22]

A tension exists between freedom and discipline. The prerequisite for knowledge is "discipline in the acquirement of ordered fact."[23] On the one hand, imagination pushes us into disorder and ambiguity. On the other hand, calculative reason orders and organizes. This is similar to the point I made in the last section concerning thinking. Thinking is at once toward order and disorder. Thinking is towardness-untowardness.

We could look at freedom and discipline in light of Nietzsche's Dionysian and Apollonian distinction.[24] The Dionysian is the urge toward destruction and chaos. The Apollonian is the urge toward order and schematization. When these forces interact, a great intellectual force can develop, and actually did develop, according to Nietzsche, in the form of Attic tragedy. Accordingly, philosophies of education must deal order and disorder.

Whitehead believes that freedom and discipline can be applied to a person's education such that they are not adversaries. At the beginning and end of our education (the Stages of Romance and Generalization respectively), freedom should be dominant. In the middle stage (the Stage of Precision), discipline should be dominant. In none of these stages should interest be killed. Even in the Stage of Precision, joy should be present. At this stage, students desire exactitude and experience joy in such a pursuit.

In the Stage of Romance ("Infatuation" might be a better term), children encounter knowledge on its most superficial level, flitting from subject to subject as bees from flower to flower. Children taste the flavors of different ideas, something like "Taste of" festivals, where we sample tiny amounts of many different foods. Whitehead warns us that education is not "a process of packing articles in a trunk," but "is the assimilation of food by a living organism."[25] The second analogy is not much better than the first and fails to appreciate the freedom that Whitehead applauds. "Assimilate" can mean "absorb," as in the assimilation of food. We must be careful, Whitehead says, not to feed children the wrong foods. The idea of absorption, assimilation, is not so different from packing things in a trunk. In both cases, you are selecting the contents to be placed in the vessel. In both analogies, the pedagogue is placing contents in a vessel. Paulo Freire distinguishes between making something accessible to students and depositing it in their minds.[26] Whitehead's analogies suggest depositing. When we think of absorption, we think of a sponge absorbing liquid. The sponge is not an active organism that seeks knowledge, nor can it synthesize knowledge. Instead, it merely absorbs its contents. The analogy of feeding a child with the wrong food also suggests a passive relationship between the learner and the object of knowledge. Yet in the Stage of Romance, freedom is supposedly the dominant mode.

The Stage of Romance is followed by the Stage of Precision. This is where students crave to know subjects exactly. Whitehead's point can be deepened by introducing David Hume's assertion that the easy and obvious philosophy must have an element of the accurate and abstruse.[27] The great painter must know the anatomy of the human body in great detail in order to paint it. This is the stage of discipline. Romance fades to the background, but remains a source of stimulation. The only discipline is self-discipline, which can be acquired by allowing the students freedom to explore. But again, imposed tasks are not out of the question. The cultivation of self-discipline is the cultivation of self-determination and the cultivation of autonomy.

The final stage is that of generalization. This stage is the synthesis of the Stages of Romance and Precision. In the Stage of Generalization, students want to utilize the precise knowledge they already possess. They want to take their ideas to the world. And this is the purpose of education: "a preparation for battling with the immediate experiences of life, a preparation by which to qualify each immediate moment with relevant ideas and appropriate action."[28] In the Stage of Generalization, the details that we learned in the Stage of Precision are applied subconsciously. In the Stage of Precision, we may learn nuances of grammar. In the Stage of Generalization, we subconsciously apply grammar as we write our novels, poems, and treatises.

Whitehead surmises that the Stage of Romance lasts for the initial twelve years of life; that the Stage of Precision spans the whole period of secondary education; and that the Stage of Generalization begins at "manhood" and blossoms at the university level.[29] In each stage, all three tendencies are present, although one dominates.[30] Education is cyclical, and within each stage we find "an alternation of dominance."[31]

Those guiding students through the three stages, Whitehead believes, should not present themselves as know-it-alls or oracles, but as ignorant people trying to fathom a little of the world around them.[32] In not presenting themselves as oracles, teachers implicitly put themselves on the same level as students, as learners. Whitehead neglects to discuss the contributions the students make to the growth of the teachers' knowledge. I don't take this as a careless omission, but as a presumption on his part that students have little or nothing to contribute. For him, the classroom *dynamic* remains teachers spoon-feeding students in an anti-dialogical setting.

3. Imagination and Holism

Whitehead's philosophy of education includes two elements crucial to the development of human beings: imagination and holism.

In "Universities and Their Function," Whitehead proclaims that a university justifies its existence by preserving the connection between knowledge and the zest for life. This it does by bringing together the young and old "in the imaginative consideration of learning."[33] Imaginative co-investigation breeds excitment and energizes the university community. The learned and imaginative life Whitehead envisions is not something we do every once and a while, but is a way of life. In the university, imagination is intensified when everybody in the university interacts. Teachers become more imaginative by doing research; researchers become more imaginative by teaching.

The ideal university imaginatively imparts information. Imagination illuminates facts, says Whitehead. He also declares that imagination energizes facts, prevents them from being inert: "You may be dealing with knowledge of the old species, with some old truth; but somehow or other it must come to the students, as it were, just drawn out of the sea and with the freshness of its immediate importance."[34]

Educators who value imagination have little problem affirming creativity and dynamism. Imagination points us beyond routine and static possibilities. It throws us toward new and dynamic possibilities. But more than throwing us toward such possibilities, imagination synthesizes. It connects those things that were previously disconnected. Syntheses are creative acts. They represent the creation or births of new pathways, new possibilities, new hopes, and new dreams.

Schooling designed to reform or to maintain the status quo cannot allow too much imagination in the classroom. This is because besides envisioning new technological tools, the imagination can also envision new social orders. Thus, it is the job of reformers not to let the imagination get too out of control.

The affirmation of the imagination also complements holism. If the imagination points to new and dynamic possibilities, then it seeks out and creates interconnections. Holistic thinking is precisely the recognition of interconnections.

Contrary to what I asserted in the last three paragraphs, Whitehead contends that faith in reason is the faith that everything is interconnected, that a harmony of logic and an aesthetic harmony exist.[35] Against Whitehead, I contend that we need not have faith in reason to believe that everything is interconnected. Imaginative acts can disclose the interrelatedness of things. But more than showing the interrelatedness of things, imagination discloses a dynamic interrelatedness of patterns of order and disorder.

4. Value and Science

We conclude this chapter on Whitehead with his observations concerning the nature of value.

Our urbanized civilization, says Whitehead in *Science and the Modern World*, is insensitive to aesthetic values. This lack of aesthetic appreciation stems from the following assumptions: (1) the valuelessness of matter; (2) the antithesis of things and values; and (3) the societal affirmation of material things and capital.[36] Added to that, within the capitalistic framework, aesthetic values have no intrinsic value, but are reducible to efficiency. At the moment the urbanized world needs aesthetic awareness the most, it disregards aesthetic sensitivity and treats art as a frivolity.

Whitehead recognizes the importance of value. But value has no place within the physical sciences: "The characteristic of physical science is, that it ignores all judgments of value: for example, aesthetic or moral judgments."[37] Value judgments "are no part of the texture of the physical sciences."[38] Whitehead concedes that human motives for creating science and for selecting which parts of the scientific field are to be cultivated are charged with value. Such value judgments may be aesthetic, moral, or utilitarian.

The physical sciences do not exclude value judgments. Phenomena that are predictable are valued more highly than those that are unpredictable. Is that not a value judgment? Valuing one kind of knowledge (that of physics) more than another sort of knowledge (that of the social sciences)—Is that not a value judgment? Does not science value truth over falsehood? Is that not a value judgment?

For Whitehead, wisdom is the way in which value is added to immediate or bare experience.[39] Value is something that is added and stirred into experience, like sugar into coffee. Experience is never value-free; hence, values are not added to "bare" experience. Value oozes from everything.

5. A Reassessment

Much as I have criticized Whitehead's philosophy of education, I must amend what I said at the beginning of this chapter. I am not deeply disappointed, but only minimally so. Whitehead realizes that spiritual adventures, "adventures of thought, adventures of passionate feeling, adventures of aesthetic experience," are more powerful than our physical wanderings.[40] Whitehead also recognizes that static values cripple human flourishing and must be supplanted by "vivid, but transient values."[41] In Whitehead, we find a holistic vision of learning in which wisdom, knowledge, and value are integrated and human beings are seen as works in process.

But does Whitehead's philosophy of education, though it recognizes human beings as process, save us from inert ideas?

Whitehead's philosophy of education barely nudges rather than dynamizes ideas. The imagination temporarily energizes ideas, but that is not the same as continually dynamizing them. Ideas are continually dynamized in dialogue, as they are batted back and forth and compel us to seek deeper and richer integrations. Dialogue is the life activity that vitalizes ideas. Thus others are essential for batting around or bouncing around ideas.

It takes a lot to "bounce around" ideas. Inert ideas can be thought of as deflated balls that don't bounce even when we try to bounce them. But even if the balls are filled with air and bounce, they will remain inert without dialogue to bounce them around.

Ideas are doomed to inertia unless they are bounced around in dialogue.

THREE

UPGRADING DEWEY

Like Whitehead, Dewey understands the mistake of equating information with judgment: "Acquiring information can never develop the power of judgment."[1] A profound difference exists between reciting facts and reflecting on or judging them, Dewey says.[2]

Like Whitehead, Dewey rejects inert ideas. In the *Moral Principles of Education*, Dewey refers to "moving ideas": "The business of the educator— whether parent or teacher—is to see to it that the greatest number of ideas acquired by children and youth are acquired in such a vital way that they become *moving ideas*."[3] Moving ideas compel people to act and escape mental servility: "The child must be educated for leadership as well as for obedience."[4]

Whitehead and Dewey also agree about the development of the whole person. Whereas Whitehead deems the development of aesthetic sensibilities as intrinsic to well-rounded schooling, Dewey sees emotional responsiveness as the basis of ethical responsiveness. Without emotional responsiveness, persons become hard and formal instead of sympathetic, flexible, and open.[5]

In believing that life in all of its manifestations is the only subject matter for education, Whitehead addresses the need for holistic education. Dewey has a similar viewpoint: "these subjects have to do with the same ultimate reality, the conscious experience of man."[6]

From my critique of Whitehead, it does not take a psychic to foresee my critique of Dewey. Throughout I condemn Dewey's reformation of education. From the radical perspective, reformation is never enough. Many persons say that a little change is better than no change. Something is better than nothing, according to this logic. In this case, something is not better than nothing. This something is the false generosity of the elites who throw bones (with little or no meat on them) to the oppressed. The belief is that somehow things will get gradually better. Bones are thrown to the oppressed to mollify and neutralize them. This is like giving me a screwdriver to cut a piece of wood when I need a saw. You are giving me the wrong tools.

I have the same attitude about Dewey's philosophy of education that I have about Whitehead's: I am half-impressed. Dewey is not profound. His ideas are simply too shallow. Before I offer a critique of some of the main ideas of his philosophy of education, let me give you a sense of the direction of my critique.

Dewey's conception of freedom is mundane. It fails to capture the horror of freedom, especially the fear of freedom as Freire describes it.

Nor does Dewey grasp that the implications of embracing a pedagogy of dynamism. The full affirmation of dynamism results in radicalism, not reformation.

As much as Dewey is pro-student, he fails to understand the relationship between the oppressed and the oppressor. He fails to appreciate the depth of oppression.

The much ballyhooed Dewey is on the right path some times, but just barely (or he is just at the beginning of it). He well understands, for example, that information is not equivalent to knowledge or wisdom. He well understands that human beings undergo continuous self-development and that education must promote such self-development. Like Whitehead, he well understands how easily ideas become inert unless vitalized by the present, the world in which we live.

Dewey understands, but not deeply enough, I'm afraid.

1. Innatism

In "The Process and Product of Reflective Activity: Psychological Process and Logical Form," Dewey criticizes two schools of thought: one that takes thought as a product and the other that takes thought as a psychological process.[7]

The product people believe that the mind must be presented by ready-made formulae. Once given these forms, students can think logically.

The process people believe that the mind rebels against logical forms. They believe in giving free reign to the impulses. Their most important values of education are: freedom, self-expression, spontaneity, play, and individuality. Dewey criticizes both schools on the same count: both misunderstand the innate abilities of the mind. Human beings possess an innate ability to infer, experiment, and test. The school of free self-expression overlooks how instruction cultivates thinking.

Human beings are by nature questioners. We continually address the world. Dewey affirms the spontaneity of the mind. This does not go far enough. In the ideology of the reformer, students are more than mere imitators, more than mere apes. Dewey says: "There is an innate disposition to draw inferences, and an inherent desire to experiment and test. The mind at every stage of its growth has its own logic."[8]

To me, all this means is that we can become good technocrats and fit within the techno-industrial capitalist world. Inferring, experimenting, and testing— these are fine qualities, but suggest nothing about transformation or creativity in human beings.

Radicalism calls for something different. Radicalism sees human beings as capable of transformation, transmogrification. A radical ideology affirms the great transformative powers of human beings. We can be anything and the world can be anything.

At the root of a radical pedagogy is the assumption of human creativity. The affirmation of human creativity as an innate quality suggests that people can be self-determining beings. Any ideology that does not recognize the full extent of the powerful creative powers of human beings is in the final analysis, despite protests to the contrary, paternalistic and oppressive.

2. Gelatinous Thinking

When Dewey talks about thinking, I shudder.

I know better.

I know much better.

Like most unreflective *thinkers*, Dewey overlooks the intrinsic messiness of thinking. Vagueness, disorder, and incoherence are to be avoided.[9] The best thinking is so-called clear thinking. The worst thinking is so-called unclear thinking. This is nothing but common sense, most would say. Common sense is what I fear most. Whatever is common is familiar. And the familiar we rarely scrutinize. The familiar becomes an article of faith. So much for accepting anything on the basis of common sense.

Dewey fears "kaleidoscopic flights of fancy and consideration deliberately employed to establish a conclusion."[10] Yet the goal of thinking is not a "deadly and fanatic consistency."[11] Fixity and "the cramped arrest or paralysis of the flow of suggestion" are not elements of good concentration.[12] Good concentration consists of a "variety and change of ideas combined into a *single steady trend moving toward a unified conclusion*."[13] Consistent and orderly thinking (good concentration) does not imply inert ideas, but a movement toward an object, in the same way "a general concentrates his troops for attack" or defense or a ship is held to its course.[14] Good thinking is characterized by constant change of place, but unity of direction. Consistency does not exclude "varied and incompatible suggestions" or contradictions. Good thinking is consistent and orderly if these suggestions are viewed within the framework of the main topic (the direction).[15] Bad thinking consists of: "Daydreaming, building of castles in the air, that loose flux of casual and disconnected material that floats through our minds in relaxed moments."[16] Vagueness represents "aboriginal sin" of all thinking: "But vague meanings are too gelatinous to offer matter for analysis, and too pulpy to afford support to other beliefs."[17]

Pulp can be defined as a soft, moist, shapeless mass of matter, but also the fleshy or succulent part of the fruit. Thus "pulpy thinking" may be shapeless, but also the most delicious. When we think of something gelatinous, we may think of Jell-O or something viscous. Jell-O is hard to eat with a fork or spoon because it often wiggles off those implements. Gelatinous thinking means that difference or contradiction acts as resistance.

Good thinking is gelatinous. Vague meanings become more precise in the process of thinking, but at the same time, they become blurrier or more gelatinous as they are related to an ever-increasing number of concepts. Holistic thinking is by nature broader-based thinking, but also grayer or more gelatinous thinking. The more holistic, the more gelatinous the thinking. The more gelatinous, the thicker or more viscous the contradictions, the richer the thinking.

Dewey contends that good thinking can change places, but not unity of direction. But can the change of place bring about a change of direction? Thinking may aim one place and end up somewhere else. The object of thinking may change because of shifting ideas, contradictions, and incompatible suggestions. As thinking shifts, so does its direction. Bad or shallow thinking is "a single steady trend moving toward a unified conclusion." Good or deep thinking allows for several different competing trends that may or may not be moving toward a unified conclusion. Good thinking is not usually "steady." Good thinking is the collision of contradictory ideas and is like collision of cold and warm air, which brings about tornadoes. Good thinking is volatile. The paths of tornadoes are erratic, and often so are the paths of good thinking. Because of these collisions (contradictions), good thinking is not always steady, but unstable and dynamic. Good thinking is not always the general commandeering compliant troops, but sometimes the general facing the possibility of mutiny. Bad thinking, because it fails to deal with contradictions or difference or deals with them only on the most superficial level, is always steady. Integrating with and energized by difference, good or profound thinking tends to become unstable. Steady thinking touches the surface of difference and never integrates with it. A certain unfamiliarity characterizes good thinking, which is the same thing as saying good thinking is the meeting of difference. Familiarity characterizes shallow thinking, which is the same thing as saying shallow thinking fails to meet difference or meets it at a superficial level.

Good thinking is characterized by the friction of difference. Dialogue is the arena for the friction of difference, as our views bounce off boundaries in the form of other dialogists. The friction of such difference is the catalyst for moving rather than inert ideas. The friction of difference is also present in the vitalization of universals. The friction between lived activities with universals produces the particular pattern of those universals individually and collectively. This represents the recurring friction between the particular and the universal.

Thinking is dynamic, but is also often erratic, moving in fits and starts. The dynamism of thinking immediately blurs it. Concepts fly together and fly apart. Thinking is a toward or untoward. It integrates and disintegrates. The object of thinking is therefore gelatinous. Thinking both resides in and wants to expel itself from gelatinousness.

Trying to squeeze out of every drop of gelatinousness from thinking is like trying to squeeze out the blood of a human body: in both instances, death results. Attempts to eliminate gelatinousness spell the death of thinking. Gelatinousness provides the impetus to more questioning. Continual questioning dynamizes thinking. The gelatinous provides ever-more opportunities for thinking to work toward and against clarification. Thinking pulls us toward a goal but also against it.

Dewey's Introduction to *Philosophy of Education* exemplifies his lack of appreciation concerning the transcendent.[18] Dewey rejects the view that philosophy concerns an unchanging being and reality that is beyond human understanding. Philosophy, he believes, employs scientific methods in its search for knowledge. This movement of philosophy is called experimentalism, instrumentalism, or pragmatism. Dewey wants to bring philosophy down to earth. He abhors all forms of absolutism because absolutes are isolated and thus cannot be judged. Unfortunately, in bringing philosophy down to earth, Dewey ignores the beyond or transcendence inherent in all acts of thinking.

The beyond cannot be expunged from the human experience. Every act of thinking is a beyond, Sartre points out.[19] By examining the nature of compartmentalization and holism, we can better get a handle on the nature of thinking. Holism aims toward completeness. It wants to view any phenomenon in relationship to other phenomena. This process cannot reach a culmination because of the infinite number of phenomena to which a phenomenon can be related. Compartmentalization lends itself to reductionism. Compartmentalized inquiry does not want to transcend the boundaries that it has set up for itself. It then turns itself in another direction, toward reductionism. It wants to find the lowest common denominator, or that to which everything can be reduced or simplified. But we never reach a final destination in the quest to simplify a phenomenon. This is like one of Zeno's Paradoxes in which space can be infinitely divided. There is no final reduction for reductionism, just as there is no final completeness for holism. Like the holist, the reductionist ends up in the same place: infinite transcending or pointing to a beyond.

As such, all thinking clarifies only to the extent that it muddies. It muddies as it clarifies. It smoothes out the wrinkles only to create more wrinkles.

Thinking is always in the beyond. So intent is Dewey on demolishing the supernatural that he misunderstands the nature of thinking. In so doing, thinking becomes mystified. Mystification can occur by making something dimmer and dimmer or by making it extremely complex. But Dewey mystifies thinking by reducing it to clarity. I love the irony of that. We normally think that mystification connotes ambiguity. In this case it means clarification. I love the irony.

Because thinking is perpetually beyond itself, human beings are perpetually dynamic. Thinking is at once an attraction, repulsion, an integration and dynamic contradictories of attraction and repulsion. The initial attraction of thinking I call infatuation. The repulsion I call despair. The holding together or integrative process I call care or love.

3. Uniqueness and Diversity

Dewey's perspective on the uniqueness of human beings and human talents, for example, is most adaptable to a radical pedagogy of dynamism.

The truism is this: human beings are unique. Hence, curricula must be shaped to fit the needs of multiple intelligences. This view must be integrated with a pedagogy of dynamism. Human beings have protean needs because they are protean beings. As we established in the preceding section, human beings are beyond themselves. In the same vein, Dewey writes: "A truly healthy person is not fixed and completed."[20]

Several comments can be made about this statement.

By the nature of consciousness, we are always beyond, thus never fixed and completed. According to many traditionalists, human beings have a nature (usually considered to be a quite horrible nature) that can never be altered. We must look closely at why traditionalists do not want to view human beings as beings-in-process. The notion of beings-in-process undermines the ossified ideology they want to prescribe. Supporting a pedagogy of dynamism endangers the very ideology that reformers (like Dewey) want to sustain. They want to play both sides. They appease traditionalists by respecting the past. They appease "liberals" by emphasizing creativity. Can the two be synthesized or does this represent a legitimate either-or-question?

If we are beings-in-becoming, tradition does not exist the way the traditionalists believe it to exist. It does not exist like a painting in a museum or a liver in formaldehyde. For radicals, nothing exists inertly. Tradition does not exist inertly. Thinking revitalizes traditions. In being revitalized, traditions change. Anything that is alive changes. That includes traditions. Anything that is thought about changes. That includes traditions.

Reformers want it, but can't have it, both ways. If tradition becomes vitalized, then it no longer is the inert tradition of the traditionalist. If tradition remains inert, then it cannot become the vitalized tradition of the radical.

But we do have a common feature: our creativity. This is what roots us in the world and revitalizes essences. This is enough to ensure that we can create commonality. The commonality that is created is a dynamic commonality involving lived contradictions. Abstract commonalities die. Vitalized commonalities can evolve simply because the contradictions have not been extinguished.

In "My Pedagogic Creed," Dewey asserts that education is fundamentally a social institution that focuses on the traditions of a society: "Education being a social process, the school is simply that form of community in which those agencies are concentrated that will be most effective in bringing the child to share in the inherited resources of the race, and to use powers for social ends."[21]

What is most important for the human race? The inherited resources and the present, not the future. Radicalization brings the future into the picture. It fuses the three time zones. The what-we-will-be is crucial to the radical. The true indicator of a radical is the trust in people to create their own futures. If that trust is wanting, then the inherited past and the present, not the future, are most important.

Education becomes inert because traditions are not revitalized and the future is not looked upon with hope. The future can only be viewed with hope if we believe in either divine aid or creativity. The first is a passive hope; the second, an active hope. The past, present, and future must be vitalized if we are to avoid inert ideas. Ideas in the present are vitalized only if the past and future are regenerated. Hope is fundamentally the attitude that everything can be regenerated and redeemed.

4. Teaching as Imposition

Let me take the following line of thought.

Teachers are imposers. That is what we are and what we do. The most benign teachers impose. We can use synonyms for "imposes." We can say "makes accessible" or "select the influences," as Dewey does. To think otherwise is naive. Curricula, texts, classroom set-up: all this is imposition. Please call it what it is. Milder or more brutal forms of imposition exist. But they are forms of imposition all the same. Even those who want to cultivate free play, individuality, and spontaneity impose their views by not allowing other forces to enter into the teaching experience. Even if I opt for anarchy in the classroom, I am imposing because I am creating a specific learning environment. Any time I create a learning environment, certain values come into play.

Yet Dewey states: "The teacher is not in school to impose certain ideas or to form certain habits in the child."[22]

Whether teachers are aware of it or not, they convey an ideology to students. Usually this ideology is that of the predominant class. Usually the ideology is passed on to students like cold germs are passed on with an innocuous handshake. Nobody thinks much of it. Yet ideology is passed on.

If even ideology is scrutinized, this is because a pedagogical style (let us call it "critical thinking," to use this popular phrase) has been cultivated and imposed.

Schooling is meant to form certain habits in students. The fundamental task for most schooling is to create a person who will fit into the society. In liberatory pedagogy, schooling does not help students fit into the society, but creates the "maladjusted" (to borrow from Martin Luther King, Jr.).[23]

Liberatory pedagogy does not create robots, but subverters of a dehumanizing society. In any pedagogy, habits are fostered. In Freirean pedagogy, for example, dialogue is fostered and dehumanization is deemed the supreme evil. No matter the pedagogy, some values and attitudes are affirmed, others are disvalued.

But can we call it "imposition" if the traditional teacher-student relationship no longer holds (the Freirean model) and the classroom is now peopled with teacher-students and student-teachers?[24] The problem concerns the relationship between the more knowledgeable and the less knowledgeable. Do the more knowledgeable, by virtue of their greater knowledge, "impose" upon "less knowledgeable"? Does the concept of imposition vanish when a reciprocity in the form of dialogue exists between teacher-students and student-teachers? If the habits fostered are those that challenge authority and transform the ideas offered by teacher-students, does that amount to imposition?

5. Holism

I am in concord with Dewey concerning holism. He is right on the mark. Dewey expresses his disgust for schooling in which subjects have been "had": "I have had French," "I have had algebra," or "I have had astronomy."[25] This means that the course is over and done with and can now to be filed away like a homeowner's manual: stuffed on a drawer, probably never to be looked at again.

Students "have" subjects because the subjects are presented as if they are complete in themselves. An insulation of subject matter prevents the emergence of cross-fertilization. In its most holistic sense, cross-fertilization refers to integrating the practical and the theoretical, the ideas of the ages with the lived activities of our own age. It calls for integrating disciplines, finding new interconnections. How can even "the most callous and intellectually obdurate," Dewey writes, not be interested when a holistic vision is presented?[26]

Compartmentalization is contrary to what it means to be a human being. Boxing in is always artificial. It militates against freedom. Thinking is a boxing in and a boxing out, a desire to demarcate, but a desire to transcend demarcation. Holistic thinking is a boxing in and a boxing out. In setting limits, we become unlimited.

Compartmentalization promotes what I call "intellectual virginity." Intercourse is forbidden with the Devil Difference. And you get so sick of your own discipline, you don't want to have intercourse with anyone in it. Holism promotes what I call "intellectual promiscuity." Intellectual miscegenation is encouraged. The more miscegenation, the better.

Intellectual promiscuity is a means to vitalize ideas and to prevent them from becoming inert. Let us remember that those who have a stake in maintaining the status quo do not want intellectual promiscuity. Intellectual promiscuity leads to making crosscultural studies that might cast aspersions on the way things are done in this society. This would lead to more enlightened persons who might question the fundamental premises of the society.

Compartmentalization lends itself to information gathering. What else can you do when you are "boxed in" except gather information? While some of this information gathering may be deemed knowledge, it is certainly not wisdom. Encyclopedic knowledge is not synonymous with good thinking. As Dewey defines it, wisdom is knowledge operating to provide a means for a better life. The better life, or better, the "good life," cannot be made apart from an underlying value, political and social reality, and the interrelationship between the theoretical and the practical.[27]

6. Primitive Credulity

For Dewey, education disciplines thought. Dewey, following Francis Bacon, recognizes four types of idols.[28] One class arises from human nature; a second from language; a third from causes peculiar to a specific person; and the fourth from the fashions of a time. Dewey also approvingly quotes John Locke's list of erroneous causes of thinking. These include passions interfering with rational thought; looking to authority rather than conceiving the answer ourselves; perceiving events in a preconceived scheme; and reverencing things, making them sacred cows.

The above are the "thou shalt nots" of thinking. The values of reflective thought are: (1) action with a conscious aim; (2) systematic preparation and inventions (a way of reminding us of consequences and ways to avoid them); and (3) enrichment of things with meanings (an earthquake means something different to the geologist than it does to the baby). According to Dewey, the first two values give us more control. According to Dewey, the enrichment of things with meaning is somehow apart from control. A meteorologist can describe a monsoon, but not stop it.

All this represents a deliberate, anal, way of reflection. In the first place, a certain credulity enhances thinking. Open-mindedness does not mean the mind is, as someone once put it, so open that our brains fall out. It means to be open to suggestions that contradict preconceived ways of thinking. A mind with all the "nots" suggests a control freak. The open mind is the mind filled with chaos and contradictions. It is the mind engaging in intellectual promiscuity. It is the mind becoming.

Reflective thinking must allow for unreflectiveness if it is truly reflective. The mistrustful mind always wants control. It does not trust itself, nor the world. I do not know how thinking can be spontaneous when such "reflection" is endorsed. Reflection of this sort kills spontaneity. It makes thinking too cautious.

This is not to say that mind should be naive. That is not my point at all. My point is to discuss the nature of reflection. Reflection that fails to reflect upon what it considers to be the standards of reflection is not truly reflection. Reflection that does not realize how the valuations and ideology are used as the criteria for reflection is not truly reflection. We are naive if we are blind to that.

"Wide-awakeness"[29] is the result of careful and thorough habits of thinking. From my perspective, careful thinking is thinking that is too tightly controlled. This represents a stranglehold on thinking. I am as much an advocate of "careless" thinking as I am of "careful" thinking and this is my reason: Careful thinking takes us down the same narrow, beaten path. Careless thinking takes us off that path and into difference. This doesn't mean that going off the tracks always leads anywhere. But it leaves open the possibility of leading elsewhere. Careless thinking is conducive to allowing for the serendipitous insight. The sudden intrusion of insight, from God knows where, is the rapture of thinking. Thinking is not always looking before you leap. It is sometimes leaping before you look. Careless thinking is as important to "reflection" as careful thinking is. It pays to be careless every once and a while. Careful thinking is careless when it comes to meeting difference.

Dewey says that learning is learning to think. Knowledge is not information, but information that is comprehended. That is all well and good. Unless we grasp the true dynamism of thinking, as the friction of difference (and that friction best exemplified in dialogue), then ideas remain inert.

7. Freedom

I will address Dewey's notion of freedom.

Dewey equates discipline as a trained power with freedom. Other attributes of freedom include:

(1) Being able to act independently of external sources.
(2) Possessing mastery not dependent upon promptings of teachers.
(3) Conquering obstacles.[30]

This represents only the most basic and oversimplified view of freedom. It does not refer to the ontological dimension of freedom nor the concrete forms of oppression that interfere with realizing freedom.

Dewey's description of freedom leaves out the notion of fear of freedom, as described by Paulo Freire.[31] Freire shows us that many people would rather have security than seek freedom. Freedom entails that people take responsibility for their actions. It means abandoning the security of traditions. It means resisting the oppressors from coercing us to abide by those traditions in order to create new value and meaning for ourselves. Freedom entails leaping before looking. Freedom entails dynamized thinking that boxes in and boxes us out from what is boxed in.

Freedom is difficult to attain for the oppressed because they internalize the image of oppressor, the prescriptions, the values of the oppressor. Traditions are suffused with these images, as in the accepted canon and commercialized ventures. Pedagogues genuinely interested in freedom must try to understand the nature of the internalization of the image of the oppressor, which "boxes in" the mind. Liberator pedagogues are holistic because they address the boxing in and boxing out of human thinking.

8. The Concrete and the Abstract

For Dewey, the concrete is the familiar and the abstract is the unfamiliar.[32] The more familiar something becomes to us, the more concrete it becomes. In our first acquaintance with Heisenberg's Uncertainty Principle, we may consider it abstract. Upon becoming more familiar with it, we then regard it as concrete. What was once abstract to us can become concrete, which is merely saying that the unfamiliar can become the familiar. Dewey warns us not see the concrete as limited to the lower end of the educational and the abstract to the upper end.[33] The concrete and abstract are relative to our intellectual development: the unfamiliar can become the familiar, the familiar the unfamiliar. Generally, the dividing line between the concrete and the abstract can be discerned by examining *"the demands of practical life."*[34] Whatever we encounter in our common social life (sticks, stones, meat, potatoes, houses, trees, laws, taxes, wages) counts as concrete. Whatever is not intimately connected with practical concerns counts as abstract. The following principle distinguishes concrete and abstract thinking: *"When thinking is used as a means to some end, good, or value beyond itself, it is concrete; when it is employed simply as a means to more thinking, it is abstract."*[35] Being able to think abstractly or theoretically and concretely or practically represents a higher order of thinking than someone being able to do one or the other. Schooling must not cultivate one sort of sort of thinking over the other. Purely abstract thinking ignores the content of existence, but when thinking becomes too practical, it narrows the scope of our vision and prevents us from escaping the routine and custom.

Concrete thinking entails actively dealing with present difficulties. This includes "intelligent selection and adaptation of means and materials."[36] Concrete thinking is an intelligent doing, which is what Dewey means by beginning with the concrete. If these means and materials do not compel the mind to leap to meaning beyond them, then the result is abstraction because the focus is on physical excitations rather than on ideas. The educational activities of childhood, Dewey contends, should lead children from what directly interests them to matters that are more indirect and remote, for instance, coloring leading to questions of aesthetics.[37] This is what Dewey means by going from the concrete to the abstract.

Dewey is on the scent of thinking, but has not discovered thinking itself. Thinking bounces from the familiar to the unfamiliar. Thinking points beyond its object. The object of thinking is always more than what is presented. Thinking consists of otherness or difference, or what Dewey terms the abstract or unfamiliar. Thinking "jumps around" and is erratic by its transcending nature. Since thinking always points toward the unfamiliar, thinking is always abstract (by Dewey's first definition of the abstract and concrete).

"Progressive schooling" begins with an understanding of the nature of thinking and does not attempt to compartmentalize it. Progressive schooling understands the otherness of thinking.

The schism between the theoretical and the abstract reflects the nature of American society. It reflects the anti-intellectualism of "practical persons" and their mistrust of intellectuals and the so-called higher education of the elites. This schism also suggests a struggle for power and influence between practical business persons and intellectuals. It portends a society in which "thinking" has been separated from "doing."

The previous discussion suggests that the distinction between the concrete and the abstract, the basis for Dewey's argument, demands "abstract theorizing" in order to be fully understood. Thus, "abstraction" is requisite for getting at the very nature of the distinction itself.

Another reason practical persons reject "abstract theorizing" is that it leads others (the oppressed) to examine the foundation of the society and who is in power. "Abstract theorizing" undermines the power of the oppressors who want to conceal the true nature of their power in order to quell potential reform or revolution.

Still another reason "abstract theorizing" is rejected is that it represents the mind at its most dynamic, chaotic, and unfamiliar. Practical persons fear the tumult of thinking and thus difference. They fear thinking because they fear dynamism. They fear dynamism because the recognition of ourselves as beings-in-becoming compels them to be responsible for creating their own worlds.

Concrete thinking involves "intelligent selection and adaptation of means and materials." Don't concrete acts such as determining laws, taxes, and wages involve "abstractions" such as justice, freedom, self-determination, and liberty? The *intelligent* selection and adaptation of means and materials is always a theoretical selection and adaptation of means and materials. Hence, the theoretical or abstract is wrapped up with the concrete. The world of things is subsumed to the world of ideas. Without a world of ideas to call things things, there would not be things at all.

FOUR

FREIRE'S RADICALISM

When I first read Paulo Freire, I thought I was reading myself or what I dreamed I could be.

In Freire, I find a philosopher who cares greatly about the oppressed. His caring is not the least bit paternalistic, but is infused with the hope and faith that the oppressed can become autonomous thinkers and ultimately free themselves and their oppressors. Love, hope, and a sense of community stream from Freire's texts. Freire's faith in his fellow beings awakened the same sense of faith in me.

In my view, Freire's greatest insight is his understanding of the teacher-student relationship as the central pedagogical issue. The goal for all of educators is to develop conditions in which teachers become students (teacher-students) and students become teachers (student-teachers). Only in a humanized and loving environment can people simultaneously become teachers and students. I develop this line of thinking to suggest that the ultimate loving relationship is one in which people simultaneously view one another as both teachers and students. Moreover, I suggest that the supreme state of knowing is characterized by the ultimate loving relationship just described. This involves a new understanding of spontaneity and receptivity. I also contend that truth emerges as a result of negotiation and integration.

Dialogue is also primary to Freire's philosophy of education. Dialogue is not possible when dehumanization is present and a traditional teacher-student hierarchy is present. I extend Freire's thought by saying that dialogue dynamizes ideas and prevents them from becoming inert.

In some areas, Freire's thought needs development. These areas include: (1) the nature of value; (2) essentialism; (3) ambiguity and the nature of thinking; and (4) difference and indifference.

Underlying Freire's pedagogy is a value system that affirms love, hope, humanization, solidarity, trust, change, commitment, holism, and self-determination. All intellectual endeavors, I contend, commence with an understanding of the value system that provides the framework for subsequent inferences.

Does Freire believe in universals? I contend that the list of values in the previous paragraph constitutes universals. Freire does not work out the relationship of lived activities with such universals. My task is to demonstrate that individual and collective creative acts conglomerate recurring patterns of essences.

Freire's conception of "fear of freedom" is too narrow. Fear of freedom as fear of breaking away from the dictates of the oppressor is but one species of a more general fear of freedom: Fear of Process, Difference, and Creativity. Human beings surround themselves with "circles of certainty" because they do not want to address the changes that emerge from their moment-to-moment thinking and living. If thinking is a transcendent act, then no moments are certain and the future is "different" from the present. By surrounding themselves with circles of certainty, people deny the true nature of thinking. By denying difference in thinking, people escape from their responsibility of defining and shaping (creating) the world. Such people are not merely acting in bad faith, but they are incapable of love. Love is spontaneous (emerging from a subject), but also receptive (to the person loved). If knowing involves both the universal and the particular, then those who fear process, difference, and creativity, can never know. Universals are only known through their coalescence with specific or particular lived activities. Finally, fear of process, difference, and creativity mars our fundamental ontological relationship with others, which consists of spontaneity and receptivity. Those who fear freedom fear being spontaneous or creative agents, but also fear being receptive to (different) others, who contribute to our creativity. They fear taking responsibility and having their responsibility shaped by others.

Freire does not address the function of difference in dialogue. I contend that a large part of fear of freedom is fear of difference. By its very nature, dialogue provides for the friction of difference. The friction of difference is inherent in co-creative activities.

Whitehead and Dewey are correct in their analyses of inert ideas. Freire's analysis of the teacher-student relationship, oppression, and fear of freedom deepens our analysis of this subject.

1. Sectarianism, Radicalism, and *Conscientização*

In the Preface to *Pedagogy of the Oppressed*, Freire distinguishes between sectarianism and radicalism, between radicals and sectarians.[1] Radicals are co-cognizers and co-creators of truth; affirmers of freedom; and proponents of reality as a dynamic complex of dialogue and action. Sectarians are purveyors of propaganda, half-truths, prevarications, lies, and myths; negators of freedom; and proponents of reality as static and unable to be transformed by human creativity.

Another way of understanding the differences between the two is to invoke Plato's distinction between sophism and philosophy. Philosophers are lovers of truth. Sophists are architects of arguments designed to muddy the waters and win arguments. "Sophist" is derived from the Greek *sophizesthai*, which means "to play tricks." Philosophers love truth; sophists play tricks. Philosophers are radicals; sophists, sectarians.

The preceding characterization of sectarianism and radicalism is only meant to present the distinction in the broadest genus possible. The next task is to examine Freire's unique treatment of this distinction.

Radicalism is at the basis of a philosophy or pedagogy promoting dynamism and cannot be understood in the abstract. Radicalism is not the destructive misanthropy of the cynical bystander. Radicalism is organic and emanates from lived activities or a particular political and social situation. Abstracted from lived activities, radicalism loses all the winds in its sails.

Radical conscience concerns itself with political, social, and economic contradictions and political action against oppressive elements. Conscience is apprehension of oppression and action against it. Radical conscience, rooted in social and political reality, does not contain an abstract concept of sin, for example, all of us being sinners for Adam's capital crime. "Being conscientious" means directing our attention to social, political, and economic contradictions rather than contrived and superficial offenses meant to divert our attention. For example, I am conscientious about the extra ten pounds I should lose rather than the rights I may lose if I am not conscientious about what President X, Senator Y, and Secretary of State Z are doing.

Radicalism is always creative and critical, says Freire. It involves an ever-increasing commitment to the positions we choose. The more radical we are, the more we enter the world. We enter reality through our transformation of it. By entering reality, radicals know it better and transform it. Radicals are not inorganic intellectuals who are isolated from the people. They are in continual dialogue with the people. They are not the sole proprietors of history, but the co-owners of it. Radicals fight side-by-side with the people and do not liberate them from above.

Freire understands radicalism as organic and transformative. Radicalism involves persons (subjects) who know and act upon objects, which are known and acted upon.[2] Radicalism is never mere subjectivism. For Freire, knowledge of the world comes through dialogue, which presupposes the existence of other subjects. Together, we co-cognize the world and name it. Co-cognition of the world or knowledge of it means acting upon it, and from acting upon it we gain knowledge.

Radicals do not surround themselves in "circles of certainty."[3] Like Socrates, they expose their views to the scrutiny of dialogue. Radicals doubt themselves. They open themselves up to difference. Because of that, they are the epitome of intellectual integrity.

A philosophy of dynamism is possible only when the status quo is constantly imperiled. This is possible when we engage in dialogue whose focal point is *conscientização*.[4] We change ourselves by changing the deepest conditions of our being, our social and political reality.

Radicals prefer liberty to security. They overcome what Freire calls "fear of freedom."[5] Instead of being wrapped in the security blanket of the status quo, radicals, guided by *conscientização*, seek a liberty that may be disconcerting and perturbing. One of the reasons we fear freedom is that the ambiguity that emerges from breaking from the status quo. Radicals, being open to dialogue and not encased in circles of certainty, may change even their most cherished beliefs. Such openness allows radicals to look at history not as stagnant, but as evolving and protean. History is open and can be changed by our efforts.

Freire does not discuss the transformation from the hugger of the status quo to the radical. It is not faddism. Suddenly, the person has a revelation and is magically transformed into a radical. Flip-flopping from position to position may appear radical, but may be another mode of fear of freedom. Faddists, for example, can slip from position to position because the herd is doing the same things they are. This is not a change of position due to reflection and action, but because of the fear of not conforming to popular opinion. Spontaneity is absent in faddists. To be a radical means to be at home with doubt. The point is not to eliminate doubt, as sectarians do, but to allow doubt to propel us to ever-new ideas and critiques of social and political reality. Doubt, arising from contradictions that emerge in dialogue and co-creative activities, is not seen as crippling, but serves as an impetus to new ideas.

Radicalization liberates because it is guided by a truth-bearing, critical spirit. Sectarianism mythicizes and therefore alienates people from the truth-bearing process, which is interconnected with social and political reality. In contrast to the critical spirit, sectarianism is irrational and mythicizes reality. Reality is defined once and for all and not allowed to emerge. It is not created by co-cognition of equals, but is imposed by oppressors.

Both leftist and rightist sectarianism is orthodoxy. Their defining characteristic consists in the negation of freedom.[6] Rightist sectarianism domesticates people in the present so future generations will be equally fangless and clawless. The banking concept of education, in which masters (teachers) deposit whatever they want into their passive slaves (students), is one way to bring about domestication. Complementing the banking concept of education in this process of domestication are strategies such as divide and rule, cultural invasion, and co-optation. For the rightist sectarian, today is reproduction of the past (tradition), and the future will be a mirror image of the present. The ruling class domesticates the people by hiding the truth from them or presenting it in a piecemeal way so as to prevent the emergence of *conscientização*. Oppressors define reality and pass it on to the oppressed, who are treated as beings unable to transform their worlds.

Leftist sectarians also prevent the people from creating history. For leftist sectarians, the future is ordained. A certain future will inevitably come to be. It is not co-created by the people. If we cannot create history, then we have no freedom, according to Freire. When we are domesticated, we are made intellectually and spiritually effete and cannot change history. Thus, our freedom is stripped from us. When the future is considered fixed, then we are also stripped of our freedom. This is because the future is out of our hands and not our own creation.

Unless we own history, we are alienated from it. If we are free beings, we believe that history is our making. History is in our own image. If we are unfree, history is made by others, the oppressors. Freire talks about naming as crucial to the oppressed, something I will discuss later. For now, I want to point out the importance of naming our history. When we create history, we name it. The events are co-cognized in dialogue and belong to everybody. This is in contrast with the oppressors naming history, owning it. Fear of freedom, if we wish to extend Freire's thought, means fear of taking responsibility for naming our history. We would rather have the oppressors define it.

Essential for our self-definition and self-identity, and thus for self-determination, is the creation of history. This is an ongoing process involving reformulation and regeneration of the past and development of our actions in the present to bring about the future. History is inert when the past becomes mummified and unassailable to critique. I am not talking about the past being subject to revisionism. I am talking about the past being revalued, a natural process of all human beings. The future can only be made if the past is remade, revalued from the lived activities of the present. The future opens up with possibilities to the extent that the past is open to possibilities.

When we cease to become history-making beings, we are prone to apathy and a sense of fatalism. Our freedom consists in revaluation of the past, which opens up possibilities for the present and the future. Our creativity as human beings is fundamentally our history-making. Any strong affirmation of creativity means that world is transformable. The world of human beings is a historical world consisting of past, present, and future. *Conscientização*, I suggest, must pertain not only to the present economic, social, and political contradictions and the fight against oppression, but to the past and the future.

2. Humanization and Dehumanization

Freire's radicalism is grounded in value. Radicalism aims at increasing humanization of all human beings, including oppressors. Radicalism militates against dehumanization.[7]

The notions of humanization and dehumanization are easy to grasp. Humanization refers to the treatment of people as subjects. Subjects know and act, whereas objects are known and acted upon. Dehumanization refers to the treatment of other people as things or objects. The classroom practice of filling up students with information without allowing them to play active and creative roles is a prime example of dehumanization.

Whenever people are manipulated or used, they are dehumanized. This is because they are prevented from realizing their full humanness, their full potential. Dehumanization is always violent. For Freire, whatever thwarts human beings from self-determination is an act of violence. Social, political, and economic actions preventing people from realizing their potential is deemed violent. When, for example, children living in poor areas receive poor educations, this can be considered an act of violence: "Any situation in which some individuals prevent others from engaging in the process of inquiry is one of violence. The means used are not important; to alienate human beings from their own decision-making is to change them into objects."[8]

Freire's humanization-dehumanization distinction parallels Kant's means-ends distinction. At root is the intuition that the ethical treatment of human beings consists of not reducing them to thinghood. In *Pedagogy of the Oppressed,* we can readily see that the banking concept of education is a prime means of manipulation or dehumanization. Students become the passive receptacles of knowledge selected by teachers and spoon-fed to them. This represents the epitome of disrespect. Respect for other human beings is respect for their right to self-determination. This translates into respect for their creativity. This prevents paternalistic intervention to "help" otherwise helpless beings. This respect is grounded in faith in the regenerative powers of other human beings. This respect is ultimately grounded in love and caring for other human beings. Fellow-feeling establishes our fundamental interconnectedness with others. For Freire, dialogue is the vehicle for interconnectedness.

Freire believes that the people have the choice to humanize or dehumanize. Yet only humanization is the "people's vocation."[9] Oppression negates humanization. The yearning of the oppressed for freedom and justice, their struggle to regain their humanity, affirms humanization. Even though humanization is constantly negated, Freire says, it continues to be affirmed by its negation. Humanization is our ethical North Star, even when it is negated. We tacitly admit the standard of humanization, even in acts of dehumanization.

Dehumanization represents a distortion of the project of becoming more fully human. Another way of saying this is that human beings are fundamentally beings who love; hatred is a distortion of our fundamental loving comportment. Freire is careful to point out that this "distortion" occurs in history, but is not the vocation of human beings. If we believe that human beings are doomed only to dehumanize one another, we quickly become cynical or despondent. We will only struggle for humanization if we believe that dehumanization is the result of oppression and not the destiny of human beings. Belief that human beings are innately good, not evil, and that unjust systems have distorted this vocation for humanization, is a presupposition for Freire's philosophical project. I would suggest that this question of human nature is a crucial one, especially for teachers, and actually directs the way we teach and live. If we believe that human beings are evil and will continually dehumanize one another, our view will be not to trust them and to construct as many barriers around ourselves as we can. Our fundamental ontological relationship with others will be mistrust, as we are not receptive to them for fear of being harmed. But we can never love others without being receptive to them. We cannot trust them to have more knowledge than we have because they will only turn it against us. By controlling the knowledge we teach them, we thereby control them. On the other hand, when I affirm humanization and believe that human beings are fundamentally good but have been diverted from that vocation, I can trust others and lower the barriers. Students are not my objects, but are beings who have the right to self-determination.

In the final analysis, the oppressed, in order to overcome this distortion and become more human, will struggle against the oppressors. The oppressed, not the oppressors, will ultimately free themselves and their oppressors. The oppressors lack the strength to liberate either themselves or their oppressors. This makes more sense in light of Hegel's master-slave relationship in *Phenomenology of Spirit.*[10] Slaves possess more knowledge than do masters. Masters live off slaves' labor, but are alienated from the product that slaves produce. Slaves understand the object of their labor while masters do not. Oppressors have knowledge of the mechanisms of oppression, for example, divide and rule, cultural invasion, and the banking concept of education. They understand these mechanisms of oppression because they themselves have been oppressed. Oppressors frequently don't believe such "oppression" exists, and often believe that the oppressed are paranoid. Only those who are directly affected by oppression and can discern the malady are the ones who can cure it. We cannot expect the oppressors, who believe that this oppression is an exaggeration or nonexistent, to be the liberators of humanity. Oppressors, even if they discern dehumanization, are not apt to change a system that sustains their superior status.

Oppressors view the humanization of others as subversion. Oppressors believe that the way of the world is oppression and that dehumanization is the primary occupation of human beings. In fact, they must believe that dehumanization is the primary project of human beings in order to convince themselves of the rectitude of their actions. If everybody is out to get everybody else, then I have justification to oppress others so that I might survive. This I call the ugly world thesis. If the world is ugly and people are ugly, then I have the right to oppress them. Since "the way of the world" favors them, they have no reason to investigate its nature.

A closer examination of the oppressor mindset reveals why they cannot liberate themselves and the oppressed. Oppressors believe, according to Freire, that "having more" is a privilege that dehumanizes others and themselves. It may be evident that oppressors oppress others, but how do they oppress themselves? Because they want to be a class that owns, they are no longer beings that are, but beings who have. By this, I think Freire means that oppressors have reduced themselves to the status of thinghood.

For oppressors, "having more" is an inalienable right.[11] "Having more" is justified because of their efforts and risk-taking. Toward others who don't have more, they have contempt, for obviously these people are lazy, ungrateful, and envious.

Class envy should be understood in the way some feminists understand penis envy. The penis is not what women are envious of: they are envious of the opportunities penis-laden people have. Class envy can be thought of in the same way. This is not envy for what the oppressors have, but envy for the unfair advantages oppressors have.

Freire shares this in common with Martin Luther King, Jr., Martin Buber, and Immanuel Kant: the cardinal sin, the capital crime, the most odious act, is dehumanization.

3. Fear of Freedom

In the first section of this chapter, I discussed fear of freedom within the framework of the distinction between radicalism and sectarianism. Now I want to discuss it within the framework of becoming-being.

Fear of freedom at base is a fear that we are creative beings. Affirmation of our own creativity entails affirmation of ourselves as responsible for the creation of our worlds. Those who value creativity know that "meeting their maker" means nothing more than looking in the mirror.

A close relationship exists between the affirmation of creativity and becoming. By affirming creativity, I affirm my own part in making my world. My world is what I make of it. I constantly re-create my world. These recreations or regenerations are the essence of my being. Regeneration roots and uproots me. The world does not have to presented to me as a map. I create the map as I live.

The affirmation of creativity and becoming means the affirmation of ambiguity because of the ever-changing field of meaning. The meaning-world we create may at one point cease to give us meaning at another. This means another meaning-world will have to be generated. The arising ambiguity meaning-world will have to be generated. The arising ambiguity between the previous meaning-world and emergent one is important for creativity. Creativity is an act incited by ambiguity. Ambiguity beckons creativity. We desire to bring things into bold relief, to make them clearer.

Is Freire the definitive philosopher of becoming? We must distinguish his notion of becoming from that of Nietzsche. For Nietzsche, all values are subject to transvaluation. No real core remains. For Freire, continued humanization represents an unchanging core. Thus Freire is a philosopher of becoming and a philosopher of being.

One issue that Freire does not flesh out in *Pedagogy of the Oppressed* is his hesitancy to allow those who have internalized the image of the oppressor, the oppressed, to meander in ambiguity. But if Freire fully believes that fear of freedom must be overcome, then allowing for ambiguity must be affirmed. Ambiguity arises as the oppressed attempt to exorcise the image of the oppressor. Ambiguity provides the stimulus for creation.

4. Space, Scope, and Hope

In the previous section, I reopened the discussion of fear of freedom. This section is intimately connected with fear of freedom as we touch on the relationship between space, scope, and hope (though Freire spends little time developing the relationships between these concepts).

In Chapter 3 of *Pedagogy of the Oppressed,* Freire contends that true dialogue cannot exist without critical thinking.[12] "Critical thinking," one of the most overused terms of our day, is uniquely defined by Freire. Critical thinking entails that thinking and acting are interwoven. Thinking does not pertain to ideas divorced from the world of action, but is a way to change reality. Critical thinking entails critical action. It involves immersion in temporality without fear and transformation of it. Thus, critical thinking, wed to critical action, pertains to creating social change. Instead of transforming reality, naive thinking represents accommodation with the past.

The brief discussion of critical and naive thinking sets the stage for Freire's discussion on space, scope, and hope. Actually, this notion is not Freire's, but Pierre Furter's *(Educação e Vida).*[13] The goal is not to cling to guaranteed space, but to temporalize space. Space becomes temporalized when human beings act upon and change it. By transforming space, space ceases to be what imposes itself on us, but becomes that on which we act.

When the universe is revealed to me as space, then I apprehend it as a "massive presence." Space is so overwhelming that we cannot act on it. Thus I must adapt to it. When the universe is presented to me as scope, I have the attitude that I can shape it. Thus, I do not conform to the universe, but give it scope.

Guaranteed space might be thought of as the ideology of the oppressors. Such ideology overwhelms the oppressed like space because they lack the critical thinking skills (critical thinking in Freire's sense) to scope it. When the massive presence becomes scoped, then it can be acted upon and changed. Guaranteed space is guaranteed certainty. Everything seemingly has its own place. No ambiguity is present in guaranteed space. When we think and create, guaranteed space is replaced by scoped space. In scoped space, universals like love, hope, justice, freedom, and self-determination are not abstractions, but are vitalized and concretized in lived activities.

The fatalism that the oppressed often feel can be linked to being unable to scope the world. When the world is revealed to them as guaranteed but static space, then the oppressed believe they have no elbow-room to etch their own insignia on it (name it). Once the world is presented as scope, as material that is workable and therefore changeable, then fatalism dissipates. We become involved in defining the world.

One way of examining scope versus space is by introducing distinction between the infinite and the finite. Kierkegaard writes: "For the self is a synthesis in which the finite is the limiting factor, and the infinite is the expanding factor. Infinitude's despair is therefore the fantastical, the limitless."[14] When faced with the limitless, we are faced with too much possibility. The infinitude of possibility overwhelms and paralyzes us. In the *Birth of Tragedy*, Nietzsche compares Jack the Dreamer and Hamlet. Jack the Dreamer, posing infinite possibilities to himself, does not act.[15] Hamlet is wiser because he realizes that to act we must narrow the scope of possibilities. Overwhelmed by the infinitude of possibilities, action is not possible. Action is based on narrowing our scopes.

Only through acting do we narrow our scopes. Action is a particular act in which we bring about one or several possibilities. Without acting, infinite possibilities terrify us. This is like when we face a situation in with a million and one things to do and don't know where to start first. We are tempted not to do anything because of the sheer magnitude of the task. Infinite possibility, as well as no possibility, contributes to fatalism. The space to which Furter refers can be viewed as what negates possibilities and also opens up infinite possibilities. When we believe no possibility exists, then we will not act. Similarly, when we believe that an overwhelming number of possibilites exist, we do not act. In each case, from either no possibility or infinite possibility, we do not act. "Scoping" is particular action that shows us particular possibilities.

Once we have scope, we can have hope. Only when the world is not seen as overwhelming and is capable of definition, then do we begin to have hope. Once the world is not an alien object but becomes our definition, then we believe it can be changed and begin to hope.

5. The Theme of Silence

When the situation is unlimited, action is nullified. When reality is taken "as dense, impenetrable, and enveloping," when reality is seen as overwhelming, then the oppressed can be reduced to mutism. Freire believes that silenced oppressed groups have generative themes that can be decoded. Groups that don't express generative thematics continue to express a theme, the theme of silence.[16]

Reading the early Sartre, in *Nausea* and *Being and Nothingness* in particular, we encounter a depiction of being-in-itself similar to the way Freire describes the way the oppressed view reality.[17] Viewed as dense, impenetrable, and enveloping, being-in-itself is undetermined. No scope is possible unless determinations are made. Through action determination emerges.

A philosophy of becoming must be a philosophy of action. Only through action can determinations be made. Equally important is space, conceived as no possibility or infinite possibilities. All possibility becomes no possibility. Possibility arises only in action, which is always particular. Creativity occurs in the particularization of space through action. Space as the unlimited denies action. Action limits space.

People who have been traumatized are reduced to mutism regarding the horrible events in their lives. Event are seen as indestructible, as what cannot be penetrated or destroyed. They take on an omnipotent air. When reality takes on an omnipotent air, then we believe that we are at its mercy. We believe we are owned by it. A philosophy of dynamism recognizes a continuum between thinking and acting. It prevents an indomitable object from overwhelming us. Mutism dissolves in the destruction of a reality taken as unchangable. The overcoming of mutism corresponds to the overcoming of fatalism. Fatalism is overcome as the world becomes ours. It becomes ours because we are able to name it. Once the world has been named by us and it becomes ours through our words, then the language of the world is ours and we desire to speak.

6. Fatalism and Inert Ideas

In *Pedagogy of the Oppressed* and more recently in his 1996 speech at "The Pedagogy of the Oppressed Conference,"[18] Freire contends that a sense of fatalism has devastating effects on the oppressed. The sense of fatalism, I suggest, is interconnected with Whitehead's conception of inert ideas. Inert ideas do not arise from particular social and political soil. They may have little or no relationship with political and social reality. Inert ideas are also unimpeachable or unassailable ideas. They are ideas surrounded by impregnable circles of certainty. Surrounded by circles of certainty, ideas are thereby rendered inert. Ideas not subject to dialogue become inert rather quickly. Inert ideas become the property of the oppressors and are then transmitted for absorption by students. Inert ideas are named once and for all by the oppressors and not the oppressed. Inert ideas are the mode through which the oppressed are kept oppressed. The conglomeration of inert ideas convinces the oppressed that everything is unchangeable. This represents the specter of space, which frightens the oppressed into inaction and often silence.

Ideas remain inert through the banking concept of education, which I will discuss in detail shortly. According to Freire, the banking concept of education consists of teachers depositing facts in the minds of students, who are forced to spit them back in exams without assessing the merit of the ideas. Ideas only come to life in the arena of dialogue, as discussants create their relationship to the objects and to one another. A pedagogy of dynamism is not possible without dialogue to invest ideas with vivacity. When students cannot name anything, they may end up in despair. The naming takes place in dialogue.

Inert ideas predominate in inert pedagogy, which is always anti-dialogical. A pedagogy of dynamism is the only way we can understand our being, our human beingness.

7. The Banking Concept of Education

Freire is perhaps most famous for the "banking" metaphor. Teachers make deposits in students, who passively receive them. Reality, as it is presented to students by teachers, is "motionless, static, compartmentalized, and predictable."[19] Inert ideas are fostered by compartmentalization and predictability.

Compartmentalization prevents students from seeing the whole. When students are given only a focalized view of reality, then they become more alienated . I would like to expand on this alienation. The alienation arises, on the one hand, from drawing solutions from this compartmentalized solutions that do not work. Education fails to develop holistic perspectives on issues. Secondly, compartmentalized education retards solidarity. We only see our neck of the woods. We don't see how our neck of the woods interacts with other necks of the woods and how the necks of the woods are similar. Compartmentalized learning narrows perspectives.

I am hard pressed to understand what Freire means by saying knowledge is presented to students as predictable. Predictability and control are virtues of science. If we can control something, then we can predict it. Whatever knowledge arises in classroom discussions arises from the knowledge deposited in students controlled by teachers. Teachers control knowledge by controlling or eliminating dialogue. Dialogue introduces unpredictability into learning. From the perspective of students, schooling that is predictable is schooling that is boring. When students enter into the fracas via dialogue, then predictability vanishes. Knowledge ceases to be inert when people are permitted to regenerate themselves via naming. The focal point of Freire's discussion is the teacher-student contradiction. When teachers and students are simultaneously teachers and students, then the contradiction will vanish.

The following list of principles of the banking concept of education is a microcosm for the larger oppressive society:

(1) teachers teach and students are taught;
(2) teachers know everything and students know nothing;
(3) teachers think and students are thought about;
(4) teachers talk and students listen—meekly;
(5) teacher disciplines and students are disciplined;
(6) teachers choose and enforce their choices, and students comply;
(7) teachers act and students have the illusion of acting through the action of teachers;
(8) teachers choose the program content, and students (who were not consulted) adapt to it;
(9) teachers mistake their authority of knowledge with professional authority, which they set in opposition to the freedom of students
(10) teachers are subjects of the learning process, while students are mere objects.[20]

I wish to begin with the end of the list rather than the beginning, because I believe that (10) sheds light on many of the other principles.

Teachers know and act; students are known and acted upon by teachers. Teachers are self-determining beings, while students possess no autonomy. Only teachers are active, whereas students are passive. Teachers talk and the students listen—meekly. Students listen meekly because teachers name the world for them. Active listening means at some point naming the world ourselves. Oppressors are subjects; the oppressed objects.

Teachers do all the thinking ("the teacher thinks and the students are thought about"). In order to become Subjects in the learning process, students must think. Generally, teachers make all the major decisions.

Since teachers do all the thinking, it stands to reason that they have all the knowledge. Knowledge is not co-owned, but is the property of the oppressors. If you relate this to the point I made earlier about history, you see more clearly why the oppressors own and therefore make history. Since the oppressors know everything, this gives them license to control the oppressed, who need guidance.

When Freire says that "the teacher disciplines and the students are disciplined," he describes a one-sided relationship. The teacher is constantly correcting the student. The teacher is never corrected by the student. The teacher-student dichotomy vanishes only when discipline comes from both sides. Teachers must be disciplined to ensure that the subject matter relates major themes of the society in which their students live. Students must discipline teachers by guiding them to what are most important themes for students If we relate this to the larger society, we must always allow for dialogue to discipline our leaders. In an oppressive society, a one-sided version of discipline exists. From the perspective of the oppressors, the oppressed need discipline to quell their inherent laziness and stupidity.

Because teachers are subjects and students are objects, then why should teachers consult with students with respect to formulating the curriculum? Teachers choose the curriculum and students comply. Students must adapt to the curriculum. In the larger society, the oppressed are not consulted about the program-content of the society. Standards are set, and the banking concept of education reinforces the attitude that the best thing to do is to adapt to them. Dialogical education encourages noncompliance. It nurtures dissent because it values everyone in the dialogical continuum as a subject.

Teachers set their professional authority in opposition to the freedom of the students. It is one thing to persuade students through argumentation. Arguments are won by appeals to authority ("By virtue of being the teacher, an authority figure, I am right"). This appeal to authority is often accompanied by respect we should "pay" to authority. Respect of this sort sustains the teacher-student contradiction. "Respect for authority" silences instead of opening up dialogue.

The banking concept of education prevents students from becoming creators of the world. Oppressors want to de-emphasize creativity as much as they can because it can endanger their place in the world. Creativity develops *conscientização* in students. The more students can be loaded with facts, the easier they are to control. Oppressors propagandize the oppressed and hope to change the way they look at the world. The oppressed are viewed as deviants from a good, organized, and just society. Oppressors want the oppressed to adapt to the ideology of the oppressive society rather than change those conditions that sustain oppression.

Whoever adapts best is the best educated person, so say the oppressors. Schooling becomes a means of domesticating people. We domesticate animals so that they will adapt to our lifestyle. We take dogs to obedience school. Domestication implies that one group domesticates another, controls them. But Martin Luther King, Jr. correctly says that maladjustment is warranted when the society is not just.[21]

The banking concept of education runs counter to Freire's fundamental ontological and ethical principle: becoming more human. "Bankers" do not possess profound trust in the people's creative powers. Therefore, "bankers" deny students opportunities for decision-making. In contrast to bankers, revolutionary educators form a partnership with students in which critical thinking and mutual humanization are the primary goals.

The banking concept of education presupposes a dichotomy between students and the world. Students are spectators, passive audience members. They are certainly not "re-creators" of reality. The minds of students are not seen as creative and generative, but as empty vessels, passively open to deposits. Bankers fail to distinguish between accessibility to consciousness and entering consciousness. Whereas revolutionary educators place objects before students, bankers place objects in students. Bankers regulate what kind of knowledge enters into students to ensure the passivity and thus the captivity of students.

Banking or domesticating education does not promote creativity and only views students as passive objects. Bankers treat students as inorganic objects, as if they were dead. Bankers are necrophilic. Such an inert pedagogy looks at consciousness in a mechanistic way. To change from the banking metaphor to the assembly-line metaphor, we can say that students are "put together" by teachers. Absent from this process is the spontaneity of dialogue. Such a pedagogy sees consciousness as static. Teachers directly deposit discrete bits of knowledge in students, who are couch potatoes, not re-creators. Such a pedagogy sees consciousness as spatialized. The minds of students are empty vessels to be filled up by "stuff." This view of consciousness serves the interests of the oppressors. They are the ones who do the "filling up."

The teacher-student contradiction can only be solved in problem-posing education. Dialogue is at the core of problem-posing education. Not one-sided transferals of information, but a community of teacher-students and student-teachers define the nature of the object. If we are to see the same cognizable object, then dialogue is essential. Here, Freire is too optimistic about co-cognizable acts leading to consensus.[22] In the banking model, full "agreement" is possible because teachers exercise totalitarian control of students. A single perspective is promulgated to passive spectators, the students, who are rewarded for conforming.

In problem-posing education, disagreement rather than agreement prevails. The more perspectives that are genuinely considered, the more the possibility for contradictions to arise. Agreement, if it comes, may be only on general principles that have been watered down to appeal to the larger group. Though full agreement may not be reached, the most important element is the process of dialoguing in which both student and teacher name the world.

No private property exists in inquiry. Proudhon once said that all private property is theft. I would like to extend that thought to schooling. Ideas are not the property of teachers: they belong to the community of learners. Through dialogue, ideas are developed within the community of inquirers. Some ideas are not "donated" to students and the rest held back. The thievery occurs in not allowing the full spectrum of ideas to stimulate thinking. By releasing knowledge that is not contradictory, we discourage inquirers from developing creative solutions to problems. Only in contradiction and ambiguity can profound or gelatinous thinking occur. Thus, the failure to release the full armament of ideas prevents ideation from taking place.

Traditional banking teachers value the preservation of culture and knowledge, according to Freire, but remain on the level of opinion and never climb to the level of true knowledge."[23] True knowledge and true culture emerge only in a community of inquirers whose dialogues lead them to co-define their world.

Ideas belong to students as much as the air they breathe. Teachers cannot, out of the goodness of their hearts, give tidbits of ideas to students, as if students were charity cases. Students are not charity cases; nor are teachers bearers of charity. Teachers cannot be "generous" when they want to be; whatever they have belongs to everybody.

Freire states that while problem-posing education reveals reality, banking education mythicizes it. Recalling Freire's description of radicalism, I understand that radicals enter the world and the more they enter it, the more they understand it. Challenges present themselves to persons not as abstract theoretical questions but as personal and compelling. Persons will respond to those challenges. Persons will see the interrelatedness of problems.

Problem-posing education is the vehicle for entering reality because it is based on dialogue, affirms creativity, and promotes autonomous decision-making. When dialogue, creativity, and autonomous decision-making are affirmed, then *conscientização* is developed.

Banking education is used to deny the oppressed access to facts. I like to think of bankers as the equivalent of the Warren Commission. Bankers want only a simplistic story to be presented. It can be an insipid story, but as long as bankers insulate themselves from loose ends, everything is fine. Simplistic teaching devoid of contradictions does not stir up thinking. Such teaching serves as a soporific. Unless contradictions and ambiguities are permitted to flourish, then nothing approaching thinking occurs. Bankers cannot allow dialogue because it invites engagement.

Freire underscores this point: problem-posing education views people in the process of becoming, "as unfinished, uncompleted beings in and with a likewise unfinished reality."[24] Education must be ongoing activity because "being human" is an ongoing activity. Equally as important as our ontological vocation is the valuing of our ontological vocation. Freire obviously wants to preserve our ontological vocation. He therefore confers unconditional value to it. Humanization is the core value of education.

Education is re-creation. It only is because it becomes; thus, it can be found in the interplay of permanence and change. Emphasizing permanence, the banking concept of education becomes reactionary. Problem-posing education is dynamic because it does not encourage adaptation to the present or a predetermined future.

When the world is viewed dynamically, then possibilities abound. Immobilizing fatalism is incompatible with problem-posing education. Instead of space overwhelming us, scopes present themselves to us. But we create scope, we are the scopers of reality.

Oppression prevents full humanization from occurring. Full humanization means full humanization for all people. Full humanization cannot occur under conditions where one person's having prevents another person from having. We cannot have full humanization unless all oppression is removed.

8. Teaching as Generative Theming

The banking concept of education is a means of manipulation and control. Students are stripped of their autonomy, treated paternalistically, and forced to adapt to the society instead of working to transform it. The banking concept of education is didacticism or catechism.

The banking concept of education is one extreme. It is purely authoritarian and totalitarian. The classroom becomes a depository of propaganda designed to mythicize and mystify social and political reality.

If the banking concept of education is one extreme, then a purely laissez-faire approach would be the other extreme. A libertarian approach to education places burden of development on the student. Teachers recede into the background and at the most are facilitators.

We are wrong to suppose the libertarian model of education represents Freire's position. Undoubtedly, he has great faith in the transformative powers of human beings. But in order for transformation to take place, students must develop *conscientização*. The oppressors will do all they can do to prevent the emergence of *conscientização*. The banking concept of education makes sure that thinking never becomes critical, that thinking never becomes active and spontaneous.

The banking concept of education is not only operative in the classroom, but in most spheres in American society. Clear but oversimplified myths must remain intact at all costs. Ideology must be easily consumable and digestible. *Conscientização* is the enemy of all sectarianism. *Conscientização* shows political, social, and economic contradictions. It casts doubt on the facile mythicized ideology of the oppressor. It creates ambiguity, and encourages a re-evaluation of reality.

Leaving students to their own devices is to throw them in a cave without a way to get out. Suckled on oppressor ideology, the oppressed have internalized the image of the oppressor and all that means: values, speech, dress, decorum. As ambiguous beings whose creativity has been suppressed in the banking concept of education, the oppressed have difficulty grasping the fundamental political and social framework of the society in which they live. The job of teacher-students to help student-teachers see the fundamental themes of their reality.

Freire criticizes "vertical" or hierarchical schooling and espouses "horizontal" schooling.[25] Horizontal schooling means that everybody is involved in dialogue. Teacher-students and student-teachers join together to seek knowledge.

Leaving students to their own devices is as an egregious form of schooling as the infamous banking concept of education. The glorification of laissez-faire education, what Shulamith Firestone suggests in her *The Dialectic of Sex,* can be thought of another means of oppressing.[26] Such a perspective, I believe, does not necessarily arise out of faith in the transformative powers of human beings, but out of faithlessness in human regeneration. The assumption is that these students are going to be failures anyway, so why bother giving them any structure whatsoever?

Freire distinguishes between teacher-students and student-teachers. This terminology suggests that teachers are the guides in the classroom. Teachers are guides who receive guidance from students. Students are guided by but give guidance to teachers. All are inquirers, but teacher-students are more advanced inquirers. Student-teachers are not as advanced. Freire never rules out the authority of knowledge. He rules out professional authority. A verticality of knowledge remains, but we could say that an interactive relationship exists between teacher and student.

This point is underscored by Freire's explanation of generative themes.[27] Teacher-students are best able to help student-teachers grasp their thematic universe. A thematic universe refers to the complex of interacting themes, the ideas, values, concepts, and hopes that constitute a *Zeitgeist.* Such themes often oppose one another and are antithetical. The primary antagonism is between those themes that dehumanize and those that humanize.

If the themes are concealed, the oppressed cannot act to undo the oppressive structures in the society. The oppressed must view the limit-situations not as impregnable barriers, but as stepping stones to a greater humanization. The limit-situations must be seen as opportunities to become more human and not abysses that lead to dehumanization. Oppressors regard limit-situations as dangerous and act to prevent them from becoming a means of liberation for the oppressed. Those who see these limit-situations as a means toward continued humanization want to realize the "untested feasibility" inherent in these situations. They want to explore, in thought and deed, the untested potentiality of these situations to liberate persons.

Oppressors are going to do the best they can to conceal or mythicize the thematic universe. Teacher-students must clarify this thematic universe for their student-teachers. Without clarification, action against the oppressive elements is not possible. Without clarification, the world appears closed to transformation. With clarification, the world appears open and capable of being transformed.

A thematic universe of no possibility is characterized by nihilism, despair, and cynicism. A thematic universe of possibility is characterized by affirmation, hope, and trust. This is not to say that the thematic universe of possibility is similar to simple-minded optimism. The thematic universe of possibility denies fatalism and trusts that human creativity can surmount the barriers.

Generative themes can be universal to an epoch or particular to an area. Freire identifies domination as the theme of our epoch (although I wonder whether this hasn't been the theme of all epochs to this date). Underdevelopment is an example of a theme particular to Third World countries. A society not only contains universal, continental, or historical similar themes, but its own themes as well.

The fact that the oppressed cannot perceive themes does not mean that themes are absent. It only means that the themes are deeply suppressed by the oppressors. The banking concept of education allows for only a fragmented perspective on reality. Critical thinking grasps interconnections and the whole. We know by understanding the relationship between the whole and the parts. This understanding illuminates limit-situations.

Yet knowing this whole-part relationship does not mean that limit-situations will be seen as possibility rather than as fatalism. Once the whole is understood, we see that the whole system must be changed in order for any significant change to occur. Seeing that the task is monumental promotes the sense that reality is dense, impenetrable, enveloping, and thus unchangeable.

Generative theming brings together the abstract and the concrete in reflection.[28] The abstract and concrete interact dialectically. Decoding a situation entails moving from the abstract to the concrete. It also entails moving from the parts to the whole and then back to the parts. Finally, decoding entails that persons see themselves and others in the coded situation. Good decoding overcomes the abstraction of the situation and presents a critical perception of the concrete.

What Freire describes amounts to a dialectical process. The first stage is the reality presented by the oppressors, the insurmountable limit situation.

This is only part of the situation. The negation of this reality is the second stage. This amounts to an analysis or definition of the limit-situation in which the whole is revealed. Finally, the whole returns to its parts and at this juncture the inquirer can grasp the nature of the limit-situation.

Teacher-students and student-teachers must be co-investigators. Teacher-students must not be seen as investigators while student-teachers are what is investigated. Student-teachers are not things to be investigated. Investigation of the themes of student-teachers means to investigate their thinking about and their action upon reality. There is a co-investigation of reality.

Investigation is not one-sided, but reciprocal. It evolves in dialogue, what I call integrating or negotiating toward truth. Assuming that teacher-students are able to identify universal generative themes, these themes play themselves out differently in different sub-units.

Teacher-students help identify the point of departure of the views of student teachers, what reality the student-teachers accept as the given. Comprehension of these themes demands an understanding of the people and political and social reality. Teacher-students must show the bigger picture to students and not focalize reality. The process of investigation is one of becoming. In the final analysis, student-teachers must think for themselves and make their own mistakes.

The primary goal of investigation is to reveal to student-teachers their "situationality."[29] Being in a situation refers to knowing how the world defines me and how I define the world. All human beings are in a situation. The more that people critically reflect and act, the more human they will become. Once we recognize one another in situations, then the denseness of the insuperable reality evaporates. Commitment arises only with the evaporation of this denseness, since commitment is always a particular action. Finally, the world can be shaped, intervention can take place. No longer submerged, student-teachers develop *conscientização*.

The objective of teacher-students is not to impose their perspectives on students, but to "represent" the thematic universe. Teacher-students articulate the thematic universe for their student-teachers.

This articulation of the thematic universe has four stages: (1) teacher-students understanding the situations of student-teachers and decoding them; (2) teacher-students discovering contradictions in the thematic universe of student-teachers; (3) teacher-students dialoguing with the student-teachers on the thematic universe; and (4) teacher-students developing an interdisciplinary study of the findings.[30]

The first stage of the process involves sympathetic understanding of student-teachers. Understanding is feeling-with, an act of caring, an opening of both mind and heart. Important, too, is establishing mutual understanding and trust. Teacher-students must not inject their values into the thematic universe. The only value that teacher-students hope that student-teachers should share is the value of critically unveiling the thematic universe. In the initial stage of decoding, the idiom, expressions, syntax, and pronunciation of student-teachers is investigated. The investigation must not be limited to the formal teaching setting, but extended to informal settings as well.

The second stage continues with a meeting of the team of decoders. Dialogue among the decoders prompts a re-evaluation of their viewpoints. Decoders are joined by student-teachers in this process of re-creation. Teacher-students attempt to discover the contradictions in the generative themes and then see to what degree student-teachers understand these contradictions. If student-teachers cannot extricate themselves from limit-situations, then they will respond to the world fatalistically.

A fatalistic world-view implies a lack of a task. Student-teachers must transcend their real consciousness, the ideology that cripples action. At the level of real consciousness, reality is never tested through action. On the level of potential consciousness, reality is tested through action.

In the second stage of the process, teacher-students select contradictions to present to student-teachers. These contradictions must not be obscure, but they should be rooted in the everyday experiences of student-teachers. The contradictions must affect student-teachers in a real way, referring to their directly felt needs. Obscurity of themes is at one extreme, oversimplification at the other. Oversimplication often occurs via sloganizing. This prevents students from finding their unique situationality, their own words for the world.

Teacher-students must create "thematic fans" so that themes flow into one another and form a totality. Only in this way can student-teachers grasp the whole. Student-teachers go from feeling their needs (when they are suppressed) in reality to finding the cause of their needs (emerging from reality).

The third stage of the process marks the return of the teacher-student to the student-teacher and initiation of dialogue. Teacher-students both listen to and challenge student-teachers. This challenge is not moralistic or didactic, for example, a "Just Say No" lecture on drugs. Student-teachers must come to recognize the contradictions themselves.

In the final stage, investigators create an interdisciplinary study of their findings. Freire believes that these themes should be classified according to the social science to which they belong. Themes overlap the social sciences, but perhaps belong in one more than others.

Investigators can here introduce "hinged themes," themes that did not arise during the investigation. Hinged themes can be used to coalesce the generative themes of student-teachers. Next, teacher-students attempt to determine the best way to communicate the theme, and then didactic materials (photographs, films, texts) are prepared. Didactic materials are permitted, provided they are subject to dialogue. Finally, teacher-students present the thematics to student-teachers in a systematized manner. These materials will not seem alien to student-teachers. They will see themselves in it.

9. False Generosity

Oppressors do not want to view themselves as oppressors. This is why they make many "generous" offerings to the oppressed. False generosity is a way to assuage a bad conscience. Freire emphasizes that false generosity is often mistaken for true generosity and is a strategy employed by oppressors perpetuate injustice.[31]

Tokens that do not wipe out the sources of injustice are examples of false generosity. Martin Luther King, Jr. Day, Black History Month, affirmative action, welfare, and the recent wave of "voluntarism" are examples of false generosity. They serve to justify injustice and act as a means of denial for the oppressor.

True generosity occurs when efforts are designed to help people transform their world. Paternalism has no place in true generosity. True generosity occurs when oppressors enter into solidarity with the oppressed. Feeling bad about their situation is not enough to end false generosity. Through false generosity, I can assuage my guilt. Through true generosity, I can eliminate oppression.

The concept of moderation complements the concept of false generosity. In his "Letter from Birmingham City Jail," King points to the moderate clergy as the foil to social change[32] Moderates speak out of both sides of their mouths and by standing in the middle, they prevent social change. By standing in the middle (or so they think), they sustain the ruling class and thus injustice. Saying that change must come slowly and that too much change would cause upheaval translates into meek, weak, and purely tokenistic measures. This is what the moderates call "humanitarianism."

Freire's distinction between humanism and humanitarianism can be examined with respect to moderation.[33] Humanitarianism is characterized by false generosity. It cloaks the vested interests of the oppressors to maintain the status quo. Humanitarianism poses as humanism, but the difference between the two can be summed up in one word: paternalism. Humanitarianism wants to maintain the vertical parent-child relationship, while humanism wants a horizontal human-to-human or person-to-person relationship.

In humanist and libertarian pedagogy, the oppressed begin to understand the power structures of oppression and seek to transform them. In the second stage, the oppressed develop a pedagogy that will permanently free everybody. Humanitarians will offer the oppressed only glimpses of the real problems in society and gloss over them. Tokens and a shallow presentation of the social and political world help maintain what King calls "negative peace," order without justice.[34] Humanists fight side-by-side with the oppressed and help bring about positive peace. They believe that power must be coupled with love.

To that I would add that humanitarian love is often unintelligent because it does not arise from personal contact with persons to determine their needs. Humanitarian love does not arise from solidarity with the oppressed, but from an abstract love.

False generosity represents another form of exploitation. Any time we prevent others from becoming more fully human, we exploit them. Unless pedagogy demythicizes the social, political, and economic world and cultivates creativity, then students are prevented from becoming more fully human. They become commodities.

In all oppression, the oppressed are sacrificed so that oppression can continue. In all oppression, the oppressed are commodities worth only something because they can be traded for something else. Persons can never be traded for anything else. Nothing can be traded for persons. Ultimate value cannot be traded for anything else.

10. The Oppressed: Persons Divided Against Themselves

The oppressed, according to Freire, "having internalized the image of the oppressor and adopted his guidelines, are fearful of freedom."[35]

What is the nature of this contradiction? Let us begin by determining its source. The oppressed become contradictory, divided beings because of being exploited by the oppressors. The oppressed are at the same time themselves and the oppressor whose image they have internalized.

The oppressed face the following conflicts:

(1) Between being themselves or being divided.
(2) Between ejecting or not the internalized image of the oppressor.
(3) Between human solidarity or alienation.
(4) Between following prescriptions or having choices.
(5) Between being spectators or actors.
(6) Between acting themselves or having the illusion of acting through oppressors.
(7) Between speaking out or not speaking out.[36]

All of the above conflicts can reduced to one fundamental conflict. The oppressed know that without freedom, authentic existence is not possible, but at the same time, fear this authentic existence. This is fear of freedom, the realization of personal responsibility. Responsibility means taking an active role in shaping the world. It means being an actor instead of a spectator. It means acting on the stage of life rather than being couch potatoes. It means speaking out rather than remaining silent. It means making choices rather than following prescriptions. It means ejecting the image of the oppressor rather than adapting to it. It means developing a cohesive identity rather than being divided against ourselves.

Women, Gays, Lesbians, Native Americans, and all oppressed persons strive to see their own image in the world, but this is difficult when they have internalized the image of the oppressor.

11. Dialogue, Verbalisms, and Naming the World

"Dialogue" is another overused and underexplained word ricocheting off the walls of academia. For Freire, dialogue is not simply the sharing of information or mere discussion. Dialogue presupposes hope, humility, trust, and above all love. Dialogue is not empty chatter, but an impetus to action.[37]

The word is the essence of dialogue. The word consists of the vital interaction of reflection and action. The word suffers when either reflection or action is absent. Authentic words transform reality; inauthentic words do not. Divorced from action, words become verbalisms, empty words (ones coming to mind right now: "liberty and justice for all"). Empty words cannot denounce the world.[38]

Upon hearing the word "exploitation," we should leap to action, ready to transform the world. "Exploitation" should signal denunciation. Zapped of its commitment to transform, "exploitation" does not connote denunciation.

Not only can words be stripped of action, but action can be stripped of reflection. This is what Freire refers to as activism. "Action for action's sake" makes dialogue impossible. Dialogue is predicated on both reflection and action. Pure action neutralizes reflection.

Our lives are nourished by true words. This idea can be elaborated on within the framework of truth-telling, trust, and cooperation. I am reminded of Immanuel Kant's *Lectures on Ethics*, where Kant says that the first condition for conversation and social intercourse is truth-telling.[39] Without truth-telling, trust is absent. Without trust, no cooperation. Truth-telling means that our deeds match our words. When deeds match words, then trust between people is reinforced and solidarity emerges. When deeds do not match words, then mistrust is created and alienation emerges.

For Freire, naming the world is a human vocation. The world changes when named. The names we designate to things determines how we view them. If the naming of a thing becomes a problem, then it must be renamed. Naming, then, is never once-and-for-all, but involves renaming. This view is consistent with Freire's view of creation and re-creation. Naming is not reserved for the elites, but for all people.

Dialogue is more than a verbal encounter among persons. It is an encounter mediated by the world in order to name the world. Dialogical encounters arise from concrete social and political reality. Dialogue can take place only between equals. Dialogists are equally subjects. This means that people cannot be denied to name the world. This rules out the elite's monopoly to name the world while silencing the oppressed.

Freire calls dialogue an "existential necessity," the way in which we gain significance as human beings. This is because by naming the world, we transform it.

Dialogue is not mere depositing of ideas, the banking concept of education. Dialogue is never one-sided, radial, in which one person is leading another. This would put one person in the role of teacher and another in the role of student. According to Freire, all are inquirers. In dialogue, we have teacher-students and student-teachers. Dialogue entails "the united reflection and action of dialoguers."[40] The ultimate object of dialogue is the transformation and humanization of the world.

Dialogue should also not be confused with polemical arguments between groups, for example, the Republicans and Democrats in the United States or the Labor and Conservative Parties in Great Britain. These antagonistic groups, sectarians at heart and surrounded by impregnable circles of certainty, are not committed to sharing the naming of the world. Creativity is a hallmark of true dialogue, which is never an instrument for the domination of one group over another.

Like King, Freire is not referring to a sentimental kind of love. Freire sees love as act directed toward other people and aimed at removing oppression. For Freire, dialogue cannot exist without a deep love for the world and for people. Naming and renaming the world presupposes love. Love sustains others as Subjects who cannot be stripped of their decision-making powers. Freire would probably agree with King that the most profound dialogue and love exists in "beloved community." Naming and renaming is an inclusive activity that brings together all voices in a democratic fashion.

Love is an act of courage. We love only in humanizing others. Freire shows that love that does not humanize or serve as an act of freedom is not love. Love throws us into the lives of others. Our love for others entails abolition of those oppressive circumstances in order to restore love to the lives of the oppressed.

Freire does not prioritize the criteria for dialogue. As I see it, love is the basis for humility, faith, trust, hope, and critical thinking. This is how I intend to interpret the remaining characteristics of dialogue.

Humility has the following components:

(1) Not projecting ignorance onto others.
(2) Regarding others as subjects and not objects.
(3) Not distinguishing between the elites and the rabble and deeming the elite the possessors of truth.
(4) Not believing that "naming" is the vocation of the elite and that the oppressed represent a blemish on history.
(5) Being open to and not offended by the contribution of others.
(6) Not being afraid of displacement, of losing status.
(7) Believing that all human beings are mortal and consequently not sages.[41]

As mentioned above, we cannot treat others as subjects unless we love them. Love never reduces anybody to an object. In this respect humility is based on love.

The kind of love Freire describes comes close to what King describes as *agape.* Such love does not discriminate between the worthy and unworthy. It is undiscriminating love. My argument against *agape* as King presents it is that love must discriminate if it is to benefit others. We can love people intelligently or unintelligently, in ways that will benefit or harm them. This is discrimination. In order to love them intelligently or unintelligently, we must discriminate.

We must know how to love unique beings. Our love must nuanced be in order to love unique beings. Love that is not directed to the idiosyncrasies of others will more likely harm persons, or inadvertently help them. Love is only undiscriminating when it comes to separating people into those who have value and those who are worthless. Love, or what I call "caring," sustains all as persons. Love never reduces anybody to mere thinghood. Returning to Freire's characteristics of humility: love never discriminates between the elites and the rabble. Consequently, the oppressed are not seen as a blemish on history.

Projecting ignorance onto others is a wonderful justification for the banking concept of education. Assuming that students are ignorant, teachers can take their own agendas and cram them down students' throats. The banking concept illustrates great contempt for students. It also justifies a vertical rather than a horizontal relationship in the classroom. We project ignorance onto others because we believe that we are superior to them. Love never allows us this superior position. Love places us on the same level as other dialoguers.

Loving persons never prevent others from "naming" the world. This would be a violation of others, interfering with their decision-making and their humanization.

Loving persons are not offended by the contribution of others. Loving persons validate other people by recognizing their contributions to the dialogue.

Love is characterized by courage. We are not afraid of being displaced when our beliefs are shown to have weak foundations, because our ultimate goal is not winning arguments but in the humanization of all. Dialogue is based on and sustained in love and love is an act aimed at eliminating the sources of oppression.

Faith is another facet of dialogue, an *a priori* requirement. Freire characterizes this faith as "intense," as faith in the creative and regenerative powers of all human beings to make themselves more fully human. Love undoubtedly grounds these people as ends-in-themselves and makes faith possible. Faith is an aspect of love. We have faith only because we love. Love lights up possibilities and is purely affirmative. Faith rides on the back of love. Love of others makes us see their best qualities, and that is the ground for our faith in them.

Faith cannot be naive. Housing the image of the oppressor, the oppressed are riddled by self-hatred and apathy. This is why libertarian education must be rejected. Their creative powers may be stultified. Anyone who fights side by side with the oppressed must be aware of the crippling effect of oppression. Yet faith in the creativity and regeneration of the people remains.

Dialogue is also characterized by mutual trust. Love, humility, and faith provide the bedrock for such trust and form a horizontal relationship between dialoguers. In the vertical or hierarchical banking concept of education, trust cannot be established. Not by talking down or at people, but in dialogue with the people, trust is cultivated. Trust becomes solidified when words consistently back up by deeds.

Without tremendous faith in the creative and regenerative powers in human beings, trust is not possible. Ultimately, our faith in the goodness of others, recognizing that their breaking of trusts is not part of an evil nature, but instead related to oppression, is the basis for trust in the larger sense.

Hope is another aspect of dialogue. Freire ties hope into the incompleteness of human beings and the constant search for wholeness. This search is done in communion with others, in dialogue. Hopelessness is a fleeing from the world. Freire calls it "a form of silence." When we believe that nothing can be done, we do not dialogue. When we believe that something can be done, then we do dialogue.

Like the other characteristics of critical thinking, hope is based in love or caring. Love grounds others as persons or subjects and makes dialogue possible. Communion with others is not possible without love.

Freire espouses not an abstract, dreamer's sort of hope ("Oh, I hope things get better ..."), but what I call "hard-nosed hope." Hard-nosed hope does not consist of sitting back and waiting, but in fighting with the oppressed. Hope moves me to fight and sustains hope.

The final attribute of dialogue is critical thinking. This phrase has become an educational buzzword usually associated with deepening analytic thinking skills. Critical thinking thereby is not seen an integral to changing social and political reality.

Freire identifies critical thinking with the following components:

(1) Thinking that does not separate itself from action.
(2) Thinking that immerses itself in temporality.
(3) Thinking involving an indivisible solidarity between the world and the people.
(4) Thinking that sees reality as process, as transformation and not as static.[42]

True words impel us to act, as Freire says. Critical thinkers are not afraid to immerse themselves in temporality. They are not afraid of getting their feet wet or their hands dirty. They are not afraid of taking political stands and facing the consequences. Critical thinkers see reality as a process and believe that human beings can transform themselves and in so doing transform reality.

Naive thinking is the antipode of critical thinking. Naive thinkers do not view reality as open to transformation, but are tethered to tradition. Instead of seeing social and political reality as an object of change, naive thinking sees historical time as a weight of traditions from the past that are the foundation for the "well-behaved" present. For naive thinking, accommodation to the "normalized" today is most important

Transformation is what is most important for critical thinkers. Guaranteed space, the traditions of the past, provide security for naive thinkers. Tradition mollifies the fear of freedom. We simply adapt to space. Critical thinkers transform space, giving it scope,

12. Compartmentalization and Holism

The more knowledge we have about one area, the more knowledgeable we are. The more we focalize and immerse ourselves in one area of study, the better thinkers we are.

The above is often called the "immersion approach" to critical thinking. The more we learn the nuances of a discipline, the better critical thinkers we are. This view presupposes that "critical thinking skills" are not translatable from one field to the next. Each discipline is unique and cannot be subjected to critique from "alien disciplines."

The immersion approach leads to isolationism, alienation, and intellectual incest. It becomes a way to insulate disciplines from outside critique. This is the fox guarding the henhouse.

If our education prevents us from seeing the whole, then we can never see the commonalities and interconnections between disciplines. Freire understands this quite well. Naive teachers present problems in a focalized way such that the totality is obscured. With respect to community development projects, the problem is broken down into local communities without examining how these communities are both totalities and parts of another totality, for instance, the area, region, nation, and continent.[43]

Focalized schooling prevents the oppressed from seeing the whole of political reality. For instance, it impedes us from making connections between the problems in our society with the problems of oppressed women and men in other places and times. It does not lend itself to establishing the similarities between different forms of oppression. For example, the similarities between Anti-Semitism and racism against African-Americans are startling. Both Blacks and Jews have been deemed sexually insatiable and intent on stealing the women of the oppressors. This effective fear tactic animalizes the oppressed. In the Middle Ages in Europe, when a child was missing a Jew was often blamed. This has happened many times in the United States, a famous case in recent times being the Susan Smith case in which a black man was falsely accused of abducting and murdering children.

No examination can be deemed "holistic" unless rooted in value. Freire's conception of *conscientização* gives us a sense of value inquiry, but his approach stops short of some vital questions. Specifically, he does not examine how the universal value of humanization is inferred from his ontological starting point. Nor does he justify humanization as an unchangeable value when values are constantly changing.

For Nietzsche, no value is permanent. Each person and each society must create values that affirm life. We are in the constant process of transvaluing. Transvaluing does not end after the Judeo-Christian value system has finally been displaced by a world-affirming value system. When any value system fails to affirm life, it must be supplanted by values that affirm life.

Freire would not opt for a transvaluation of all values. The continued humanization of ourselves and others is the fundamental value of Freire's philosophy. Orbiting this value are related values like love, hope, faith, and trust.

Transvaluation should be seen as identical to the notion of the incompleteness of human beings. We must continually transvalue because of our incompleteness as human beings. Assuming that values are at the core of the human enterprise, we may say that our incompleteness as human beings refers to the incompleteness of values. Denial of transvaluation amounts to denial of the human project. To be a seeker of truth, transvaluation is imperative. To promote a pedagogy of dynamism, transvaluation is necessary.

The question becomes: Are there any values that cannot be transvalued? For Freire, the answer is yes. Human beings are incompleteness. This is Freire's ontological position. Dehumanization prevents people from working toward completeness. Humanization aids them in this quest. Freire's categorical imperative, the fundamental value in his ethics, is humanization of all. This value cannot be transvalued.

Who is right: Nietzsche or Freire? Nietzsche's philosophy is pure becoming. Of all western philosophers, Nietzsche feels the most kinship with Heraclitus. Yet he cannot fully accept the Heracletian world view because of the assumption that Logos that runs through all things. For Nietzsche, everything is surface. "Beneath" and "Beyond" are metaphysical mirages. Two points must be made. For both Nietzsche and Freire, transvaluation is not without a purpose. For Nietzsche, transvaluation is integral for the affirmation of life. For Nietzsche, affirmation of life is the highest value; nowhere do I find him saying anything to the contrary. For Freire, transvaluation is integral for the humanization of all. In both cases, transvaluation rests on the base of an axiological assumption.

My argument is that human experience is never value-free. Human inquiry is based on the assumption that truth is a value and falsehood is a disvalue. At the base of all inquiry is the assumption of truth as the higher value than falsehood (and Nietzsche talks about the value of truth). If we assume that metaphysics is the basis for all other inquires, there, too, we have made a value judgment: the most general principles are the most important.

13. Subjectivity and Objectivity

Radicalism is rooted in the intrinsic interdependence of subjectivity and objectivity. In the Preface of *Pedagogy of the Oppressed*, Freire proclaims that radicals are never subjectivists.[44] For radicals, the subjective exists only in relation to the objective. The knowing and acting (the subjective) is united with the objective (the known and the acted upon) in a dialectical relationship.

Radicals are never subjectivists because subjectivism and psychologism form the basis for solipsism. Let us examine the implications of this position. If I doubt that the world and people in it are real, then I am not going to be inclined to act to change that world. If I assume that the world and others are real, then I am much more inclined to act. The humanization of others presupposes the objective transformation of reality. If objectivity is doubted, then no "objective transformation" can emerge.

Subjectivism can be employed as an ideological tool. This is the case when the ruling class rationalizes an objective fact like oppression. The fact is not denied, but seen differently, for example saying "Everybody experiences oppression in one way or another," instead of pointing to the powers that create this oppression. The fact loses its objective base and becomes a myth defending the interests of the ruling class.

Affirming objectivism and denying subjectivism is also a mistake.[45] This amounts to a denial of human creativity in shaping the world. There can be no world without thinkers, nor thinkers without a world. Can objectivism be employed as an ideological tool, in the same way subjectivism can? By segregating subjectivity from the world, we deny that the world can even to reached by our creativity. If the world cannot be acted upon, then it cannot be transformed. In this way, subjectivity becomes alienated from objectivity. Freire correctly describes how the assumption of the fictitiousness of the world prevents people from transforming it. Likewise, the assumption of a subject who cannot reach the world prevents people from transforming it.

But other problems arise from this assumption. (1) Pure objectification brands everything, including people, as objects, not as subjects. (2) Individuals remain detached and independent of other people and this prevents dialogue from occurring. (3) So-called value-free inquiry impedes understanding the nature of value and ideology.

14. Anti-Dialogue: Conquest, Divide and Rule, Manipulation, and Cultural Invasion

Dialogue is central to Freire's pedagogy. Dialogue is also at the heart of a pedagogy of dynamism. Dialogue, as described by Freire, animates ideas, prevents them—to use Whitehead's terminology—from becoming inert. Dialogue also prevents ideas from the being owned by an elite class. Dialogue presupposes that everybody can name the world.

Anti-dialogue, the banking concept of education, fosters inert ideas. Ideas come from a central source and are embedded into passive recipients. A vertical, not a horizontal relationship, exists in the banking concept. The banking concept of education regulates how ideas enter into the minds of students. Student passivity is cultivated and desired. The banking concept of education must be narrow and preach compartmentalized or focalized learning. This is strategic. The more focalized, the easier to control. Holistic thinking is dangerous to the banking concept of education. It opens up many cans of worms. Holistic thinking opens up the larger world. The larger world is exactly what the banking concept wants to prevent the oppressed from seeing.

Anti-dialogical education rests on four fundamental strategies: conquest, divide and conquer, manipulation, and cultural invasion.

A. Conquest and Unfair Housing Practices

The unbecoming pedagogy of anti-dialogue aims at conquering students. The agenda of teachers is force-fed to overly pliant students. In the classroom conquest is usually not accomplished by overtly repressive means, like patients restrained by attendants whose mouths are pried open as medicine as is shoved down their throats. Teachers could get sued for that. Classroom conquest is accomplished by subtle means. Developing a paternalistic relationship with students is one way of accomplishing this goal. The grading system is another means of control. Frightened of failure, students conform to the teachers' standards. Grades hang over the heads of students like guillotines. How in the world can this encourage creativity and independent thinking when it could lead to academic death?

Many people talk about education in terms of obtaining and storing information. This is supposed to be a good thing. But more than information is being deposited into students. Oppressors (teachers) impose themselves on the oppressed (students). Instead of treating students as subjects, oppressors treat them as if they were dead meat to be consumed. The oppressed are consumables. In addition to all the wonderful information they receive from their teachers, students also receive the image of the teacher.

They internalize the image of the oppressor. This I call an unfair housing practice. On the one hand, the oppressed want to develop their self-identity. On the other hand, because of internalizing the image of the oppressor, the oppressed are torn between seeking their freedom and abiding by the standards of the oppressor.

Freud's famous "Oedipus Complex" describes the boy wanting to murder his father and sleep with his mother. I wish to understand the Oedipus Complex in light of Freire's notion of housing the other. The Oedipus Complex should be seen within the framework of the oppressor-oppressed situation. The boy does not necessarily want to kill his father. The boy wants to rid himself of the image of the oppressor, of his father's values and world-view. The boy wants to develop his own way of seeing the world, of naming it, as Freire says. The child wants autonomy in decision-making. The boy does not want to kill his father, but the image of the oppressor.

Anti-dialogue is a means of oppression and of the preservation of oppression. It strips the oppressed of their "word" and their culture. Anti-dialogue and oppression occur simultaneously, just as dialogue and liberation occur simultaneously.

All conquest is anti-dialogical. The oppressed are prevented from considering the world. Oppressors can never prevent the oppressed from thinking, but they can determine what is thought about subject matter. By mythicizing the world, oppressors circumscribe thinking. Mythicization may not be outright lying, but it does involve glossing over truth or revealing selected truths. In any case, truth is trivialized. When the oppressed believe that truth cannot be known and will always be controlled by the ruling class, then truth is trivialized. The oppressed become apathetic because the truth cannot be revealed. They feel powerless to discover the truth. This is because they do not feel the creative power within themselves to find the truth.

Dialogue is the pursuit of truth. Pursuing the truth and truth-telling are also interrelated. The more valued truth-telling is, the more valued the pursuit of truth. When word does not correspond to deed, then words are reduced to verbalisms. Verbalisms do not impel people to action, to the transformation of the world. True words impel people to action.[46] Truth-telling involves the correspondence of deed to word. I pursue the truth only when I believe that the world can be transformed by truth-telling. When I believe that the world cannot be transformed by truth-telling, then I do not pursue truth.

Promoting passivity among the oppressed should also be understood in light of fatalism. The more the world, political and social reality, is shown as unchangeable, the less students believe they can change it. The message is: nothing can be changed, so adapt to it.

The passivity of the oppressed must be maintained. Core myths such as the following are essential to maintaining the oppressed:

(1) The myth of the free society.
(2) The myth that people are free to work where they want and they can work elsewhere if they do not like their employers.
(3) The myth that society respects human rights.
(4) The myth that anyone can become an entrepreneur.
(5) The myth that the street vendor and the factory owner are equally entrepreneurs.
(6) The myth of the universality of education.
(7) The myth of equality of education.
(8) The myth of the oppressor classes as defenders of the "true" faith against material barbarism.
(9) The myth of the charity and generosity of the elites.
(10) The myth that the elites promote the advancement of the oppressed and that the oppressed must show gratitude toward them.
(11) The myth that rebellion is a sin against God.

(12) The myth that private property is essential to human develop-
     ment.
(13) The myth of the industriousness of the oppressor versus the indo-
     lence of the oppressed.
(14) The myth of the natural superiority of the oppressors and the
     natural inferiority of the oppressed.[47]

These (or forms of these) are the myths that students swallow on a regular
basis. These myths are rarely challenged. How can they be? In the banking
concept of education, nothing is challenged. The myths are disseminated not
only in formal education, often unwittingly by well-meaning educators, but
also, and probably more effectively, by the media in many ways. No matter:
in the final analysis, few are inoculated against this inculcation.

This list of myths is not simply applicable to Freire's Brazil, but is
adaptable to any society. Make people believe they live in a free society, and
then why would they try to transform it? We're free, aren't we, or at least
freer than those poor slobs in totalitarian countries? "Freedom" is often taken
at face value and never really examined, for example, in asking the question if
economic freedom (and economic equality) is absent, can equality be realized
in any part of the society?

The second myth and fourth myths are related to the first, the myth of
freedom. Why transform the work world when I have the freedom to work
anywhere I choose? Why transform the work world when I, like anyone else,
can become an entrepreneur? I have as much chance as any other person. The
fact that I have as much a chance as anyone means that everyone, from the
CEO of General Motors to the guy who sells pens at the corner, is essentially
the same.

Other cornerstone myths include the myth of the universality and equality
of education. In the United States, while we might acknowledge that some
people have better schooling than others, we might say if they worked hard
enough, they could overcome adversity.

Another important myth is the "Us versus Them" dictum. We are the holy
and good ones, while the others are unholy barbarians who want to ruin our
way of life. God is on our side while the others are demonic.

Believing that elites are generous and that they promote the advancement
of the oppressed is to advance the idea of biting the hand that feeds you.
However, if the oppressed actually knew what kind of poison the elites fed
them, they would bite off their hands along with anything else they could sink
their teeth into.

Rebellion is considered disrespect and utter nonsensical idealistic hogwash.
Any challenge to the view of someone in power may be deemed rebellious and

disrespectful to authority. Any way, what does it matter? We cannot change anything anyhow (Freire's notion of fatalism).

The values of competition, selfishness, and exploitation complement the assumption of private property. These values support the ideology of the oppressors.

The myths of the industriousness and the superiority of the oppressors versus the indolence and inferiority of the oppressed encourage the oppressed to become like their oppressors. The oppressed become filled with self-hatred, oppressing their own people while internalizing the image of the oppressors.

These myths do not appear accidentally or intermittently. They form a network of pervasive ideology from which there is no escape. The oppressed are not only ghettoized with respect to their living arrangements, but they are ghettoized intellectually and spiritually.

B. Divide and Rule: The Oppressors' Golden Rule

The minority of oppressors cannot allow unification and solidarity among the oppressed. Unity, organization, and struggle, essential for the humanization of the oppressed are deemed dangerous by the oppressors. Subtle and unsubtle divide and rule tactics, whether through government bureaucracy, the mass media, or education, split minorities asunder and pit them one against the other.[46]

Some educators inadvertently divide and rule by examining problems not in their totality, but in a focalized way.[47] Looking at an issue in a focalized way, the oppressed never understand how this issue interconnects with the larger social and political reality, whether that be with neighboring towns, neighboring countries, the continent as a whole, or the world.[48] People become alienated from one another, not knowing that others experience common experiences and common oppressors. They suffer from what I call the "the freakness of uniqueness" syndrome. They are so alienated that they believe that no one can understand them. They see themselves as freaks, utterly different from others.

Oppressors cannot allow for a pedagogy of dynamic integration. This would lead to intellectual and social interconnectedness. Schooling must be focalized so that the minds of students are focalized. Focalized minds are the same as narrow minds and such narrow-mindedness is beneficial to the oppressors.

In the classroom, grades are a divide-and-conquer strategy. They divert attention from course content to criterion employed for judging that content. Receiving rewards becomes more important than educational enrichment. Grading turns student against student much the same way private property turns owner against owner.

Oppressors promote only selected leaders from the oppressed classes, not the oppressed as a group. Instead of having leaders and the oppressed group cooperating to expunge the source of oppression, oppressors promote a leader. But this does nothing to transform the fundamental sources of oppression.

Oppressors preach that harmony must exist between the owners and the workers. Harmony of this sort is like a forced smile in the face of a rapist. The myth of harmony is a mechanism of denial on the part of the oppressors. If they can deny they are oppressors, then, of course, no oppressed exist. If no oppressed exist, then can we really claim class conflicts exist? Apparently, Freire contradicts himself when he says that the oppressors preach an impossible harmony between themselves (who dehumanize) and the oppressed (who are dehumanized).[49] We can harmonize this apparent contradiction by saying that oppressors do both. When it is to their advantage to have harmony, they will preach it. When it is not in their interests to have harmony, then they will say that harmony is impossible. Rhetoric along these lines might include that "There will always be war" or that "Human beings will always be selfish."

Co-optation is a fundamental divide and rule strategy.[50] Those who are "well behaved" are promoted. The promotion of a few of the oppressed validates the "anybody can make it if they try" propaganda. Those of oppressed who do make it or want to make it are pitted against the lazy, stupid bastards who aren't the "good ones." Those who don't want to be "promoted" face repercussions. Not accepting the invitation of co-optation could mean being blacklisted or losing their jobs, for example.

Part of divide and conquer is the myth that the oppressors are actually the saviors of the oppressed group. The false generosity of the oppressor might be the result of guilt. Oppressors ease their consciences through false generosity. Instead of creating justice for everyone, oppressors seek "inner peace" for themselves.

These "saviors" try to convince the oppressed of their noble intentions. Marginals, rowdies, and enemies of God (demonized and dehumanized individuals) are the problem. The oppressors are needed to protect the oppressed from these aberrations, which the oppressors largely create in their alienated society. This rhetoric, like all divide-and-conquer rhetoric, is designed to deflect attention from the true source of oppression and to demonize and demoralize leaders who seek unification and solidarity.

C. Manipulation

Divide and conquer tactics and conquest can be defined as forms of manipulation. But Freire has a specific connotation for manipulation.

Manipulation refers to the model that the oppressors offer to the oppressed as means for their ascent.

The centerpiece of this manipulation is pacts between the oppressed and oppressors. These pacts are always in the interest of the oppressors. Manipulation in the forms of these pacts is not necessary when the oppressed are completely suppressed. Only when the people begin to think and organize is manipulation necessary.[51]

Manipulation can be offset only when revolutionary organizations can help the people see the generative themes of their oppression. The people must develop revolutionary or class consciousness.

The promise of reform is but another means of manipulation. Reform, as I mentioned in my critique of Whitehead, is nothing but a shuffling around and not an essential change. Essential transformations only occur in radicalization. Reform is the canned music of gradualism. Even the best intentioned cannot bring about "reform" without at first expelling the image of the oppressor.

Leaders who are intermediaries between the oppressed and the elites end up being manipulated by the elites. This "amphibian" moves between the oppressed and oppressors.[52] Such a person bears the mark of both groups and when all is said and done does nothing to eradicate oppression.

D. Cultural Invasion

Cultural invasion refers to stifling the creativity and expressiveness of the oppressed. Invasion may be physical or overt (like a club over the head) or friendly (as when in the United States white persons advise black persons to stop acting "black" for their own benefit). The oppressed internalize the values of the oppressors and eventually see the world from the perspective of the oppressors.[53]

Cultural invasion cannot occur without the oppressed being convinced of their inferiority. A feeling of inferiority is prerequisite for cultural invasion. They contrast their inferiority with the superiority of the dominant class. Everywhere they go, their society negates them, so they are rife for invasion. The oppressed gravitate toward the values and way of life of the oppressed because they are convinced of the superiority of their own values and way of life.

Radicalism is requisite for overcoming these myths. Radicalism is a pedagogy of dynamism characterized by regeneration. The oppressed must develop a means for overcoming cultural invasion. They must obtain these means through thinking and action. Instead of being nourished by the poison of the oppressor, the oppressed must nourish themselves.

By expelling the invader, the oppressed can finally have human relationships with other human beings. The oppressed are houses divided against themselves. Once the house is not divided, then we can have loving relationships with others.

Renouncing myths is traumatic. It is as we are renouncing ourselves, since *we are our beliefs*. Renouncing cherished beliefs is akin to cutting off an appendage. It can feel like form of self-mutilation. Rather than renouncing the myths, the oppressed prefer to deny reality. Rather than burst the bubble of these myths, the oppressed prefer to blame teachers for "manipulating" them to see the world in another fashion.

Science and technology can either liberate or oppress. They can be a means of manipulation, serving as a model for mechanization and making people into cogs in the machine. They can also be a means of liberation, offering ways to eliminate poverty and pollution. To assure that science and technology contribute to the humanization of all, schooling must develop *conscientização*. A holistic political and social awareness, focusing on value and ideology, must pervade the curriculum.

A pedagogy of dynamism must allow for the becoming of each individual in the society. No segment of society, no person, can be inhibited from becoming, self-determination. Full self-actualization for all cannot occur in an anti-dialogical society of manipulation, cultural invasion, conquest, and divide and rule.

Manipulation, cultural invasion, conquest, and divide-and-conquer strategies prevent humanization. The humanization to which Freire subscribes implies that all persons be regarded as subjects. This means that all forms of oppression must be eliminated. Just as pollution affects everybody, so does oppression.

Who are the invaders? They come in all shapes and forms. Not simply are the factory owners or the government the oppressors. Professors, factory workers, priests, educators, and even revolutionaries can be invaders. The image of the oppressor is found virtually everywhere in an oppressive society, in commercials, greeting cards, textbooks, and even in this book. Oppression touches everything, distorting it.

Cultural invasion consists of:

(1) A parochial view of the world.
(2) A static world view.
(3) One world-view imposed upon another.
(4) The superiority of the invader and inferiority of the invaded.
(5) The imposition of the values of the oppressors on the oppressed for the purposes of control.[54]

A parochial view of the world insulates a world-view from criticism. A "superior" world view need not be challenged by any "inferior" viewpoints.

Assuming the world is static means that it cannot be acted upon. Only when the world is assumed to be dynamic is it open to change. But the invader wants the oppressed to believe that the world cannot be changed. This assures that the oppressors remain entrenched in power.

Parochialism does not allow for difference. Parochialism lends itself to the imposition of one world-view upon another because it does not take seriously the legitimacy of "alien" perspectives.

Parochialism assumes that a superiority of one view and the inferiority of the another. This further justifies invasion (Christianity versus the heathens).

Imposing values is like imprisoning the oppressed. Circumscribed by the invader's values, the oppressed are riddled by great guilt and doubt as they struggle to rebel.

Understanding how oppression is manifested in the classroom and in other social contexts is one of the great strengths of Freire's pedagogy. Other strengths include the premises that reality is dynamic and that human beings can transform reality and themselves. Yet another strength is his recognition that love, faith, hope, and trust are vital to dialogue and to schooling. In the next chapter, I intend to build on Freire's strengths and construct and radical pedagogy of dynamism that addresses the issues of value, essentialism, ambiguity, and difference and indifference.

FIVE

A RADICAL PEDAGOGIC
CREED OF DYNAMISM

The remainder of the text will introduce a radical pedagogy of dynamism. Readers will no doubt see the influence of Paulo Freire. I have no reason to conceal the huge debt I owe this great thinker. But readers will realize that I go in my own direction. I push beyond Freire by discussing the ontological and ideological dimension of value. I develop a philosophy of education in which value stands at the forefront.

Freire discusses "fear of freedom," but not how fear of freedom consists of fear of ambiguity, doubt, and process. I explain the nature of doubt within the framework of self-consciousness, working from many of the insights of Jean Paul Sartre. I stress that ambiguity is essential for thinking and that reductionistic clarity can be toxic to thinking.

Another area in which I spend much time concerns the relationship of difference and indifference. A pedagogy written at the end of the twentieth century must examine this question, because this issue is a philosophical and societal concern. I distinguish between "having differences" and "being different" and examine the relationship between difference and indifference.

As has been the case in my earlier works, I attack common conceptions of respect and develop a concept of respect that fits a radical pedagogy of dynamism. Respect, I believe, should be accorded to obscenity. I attack the hallowed concept of respect and also common sense, which I do not condone, but for which I have the deepest disrespect.

One of the key points in this pedagogy is "trust in creativity." I draw a correlation between trust in creativity and trust in becoming. Becoming can be affirmed only to the extent we are armed with creativity. Without creativity, becoming becomes a peril to us. This is a point I owe to Nietzsche.

Yet the affirmation of dynamism is not so easy as affirming the universe as dynamism. I contend that affirmation of dynamism must begin with the affirmation of the process of thinking. Once thinking has been affirmed and we recognize that doubt sits on the edge of all belief and see that belief rests beneath all doubt, then we can affirm the dynamism of thinking, its incessant constructing and deconstructing. Affirming the dynamism of thinking is requisite for affirming the dynamism of the universe.

Once more, I take my shots at reform. The best reformer in the world can do nothing to change the foundations of education or the foundations of society.

Genuine thinking is philosophy itself. Any pedagogic creed without this point is nothing but a pseudo-creed.

Philosophy is promiscuous because it demands continual dialogue with others. One of the more controversial points I make is that we can best cultivate multiculturalism by examining the "differing" of thinking rather than by examining the "differences" in disparate groups of people.

Before I proceed to the pedagogic creed, I will enumerate the dicta that summarize my philosophy of education. Below is a thumbnail sketch of my views so that my misinterpreters will not be inconvenienced by the need to read the whole creed.

DICTA OF A RADICAL PEDAGOGIC CREED OF DYNAMISM

1. You can never piss in the same river.
2. We are always ahead of ourselves.
3. Indifference is the strategy to reduce the irreducible nature of thinking.
4. We are all Sobjects.
5. Teaching and learning is not a relationship between the spontaneous and the receptive.
6. The "impossible" is an ideological tool used to conceal possibilities.
7. The invisible is possible (for all my friends who believe in God, the soul, and that paraphernalia).
8. The nature of self-consciousness is both rooting and uprooting.
9. Sobjects are contrary to inert ideas.
10. Values are the bare essentials.
11. Something is not always better than nothing .
12. Learning is learning to rebel.
13. The greatest faith in myself and others is in our creative powers and our ability to think.
14. I am committed to others to the extent that I trust them to be creative and therefore self-determining beings.
15. Trust in the innate qualities of others should be tinctured by the recognition of oppressive forces that prevent the emergence of innate qualities.
16. Ambiguity is not a disease to be wiped out, but a cure for the toxin of narrow clarity.
17. History is not private property.
18. Cut off the hands of false generosity.
19. The more we interpret, the more we negotiate.
20. Writing the birth announcement for philosophy means writing the obituary for religion.
21. Philosophy is always promiscuous.
22. Radical pedagogy accepts only certain forms of respect.

23. Reserve respect for the obscene.
24. Triviality is the bastion of inert ideas.
25. Only thinking is allowed; thought on your own.
26. Making room for thinking means the exodus of all icons.
27. The more creative we are, the more hopeful.
28. Alienation is not a fact of life, but a fact of oppression.
29. It all depends what we are conscientious about.
30. Every human act involves teaching and learning; thus our fundamental ontological relationship with others is as both teacher and student.
31. Initiation culminates in peace.
32. Compartmentalized thinking stifles dynamism.
33. Having differences is not the same as being different.
34. When you kill spontaneity, you kill thinking
35. Faith in error is faith in the spontaneity of thinking.
36. God is the only being who is close-minded.
37. Never wish common sense on anybody.
38. We can suspend students, but not judgments.
39. Freedom is philosophy.
40. We affirm dynamism by affirming thinking.
41. Truth is compatible, and only compatible, with radicalism.

1. Cosmic Becoming: You can never piss in the same river.

The universe is in flux, and we must react and adjust to this universe in order to survive and flourish. A pedagogy of dynamism begins with the observation of cosmic change. Our observation of cosmic change makes us recognize the fragility and transitory nature of existence. A pedagogy of dynamism begins in the common observation of the world. We observe the fragility of life and the cycles of life and death not only within our species but among others as well.

A radical pedagogy of dynamism takes its point of departure in our common observations about the world and in the physical sciences' assertions concerning the nature of the universe.

While our pedagogy of dynamism begins with observation and science, it does not conclude there. The conclusions we reach about the physical world lead us to examine the nature of our own self-consciousness. If the universe is in flux, then is our thinking?

All pedagogies should be interested in the nature of our self-conscious, or what is the same thing, the nature of our thinking. A pedagogy of dynamism may take a clue the physical universe, but its focus is primarily on our thinking.

2. Self-Consciousness as Dynamism:
We are always ahead of ourselves.

Human beings, by the nature of their self-consciousness, are dynamic. We are always beyond ourselves. Thinking always transcends the immediate. Thinking points us beyond. Thinking is always dynamic. Any thinking about an object pushes us beyond that object.

Thinking is dynamic because of the nature of our self-consciousness. Because we think, we can never look on an object as it is. We must also look at an object for what it is not. This means, as Jean-Paul Sartre points out, that all belief is disbelief or doubt.[1] Doubting is not something that happens to people who lack faith. Doubt slips into all belief. We can never totally believe anything. Seeing is believing and not believing, or doubting. A measure of doubt always slips in. The attempted (I say attempted, because it can never be successful) expunging of doubt is not possible. We are beings who always doubt ourselves. This has nothing to do with a lack of self-confidence, but refers to the nature of thinking.

The expulsion of belief is not possible either. Even radical doubting cannot expel belief. Even if I doubt everything, I cannot deny that I believe that I doubt.

Thinking is believing and doubting. We are believers and doubters.

If we are believers and doubters, then everything is open to questioning. Questioning is our fundamental nature. We cannot help question any more than things in the universe cannot help becoming. Thinking is dynamic because it can never settle on one spot.

Questioned belief becomes doubt. Questioned doubt becomes belief.

Questioning is our fundamental posture in the world. We must question things in order to survive and ultimately to flourish. But this does not address the basis of this questioning, which resides in our very self-consciousness. We are beings for whom everything is thrown into question.

3. The Irreducible and Indifference: Indifference is
the strategy to reduce the irreducible nature of our thinking.

Thinking moves in two basic directions.

Thinking moves toward holism or reductionism. In the end, they are the same.

When thinking moves toward holism, it attempts to understand a phenomenon according to its relationship with all other phenomena. The attempt to contemplate all possible relationships to the phenomena ultimately destroys our understanding of the phenomenon by blurring it with complexity.

When thinking moves toward reductionism, it attempts to reduce everything to a simple one. But the simple one has no relationship with anything else. For if it did, it would not be the simple one. Not having a relationship with anything else blurs the phenomenon by simplicity. The clearness of simplicity is actually opaqueness because isolating the simple from everything else robs it of its meaning.

In both cases, thinking becomes opaque. Opaqueness suggests no boundaries. Thinking can only become ambiguous in the interaction between the reducible and irreducible. Ambiguity suggests blurry boundaries.

Reductionistic thinking is indifferent to interconnectedness. Its goal is to compress meaning into the one.

Holistic thinking is indifferent to the one. It wants to expand interrelationships to infinity. Its goal is to expand meaning without limit.

Thinking is the tension between the reducible and irreducible.

4. Sobjectivity: We are all Sobjects.

Philosophers have labored too long with the distinction between subjectivity and objectivity.

Philosophers such as Hegel and Husserl have argued that we cannot talk about subject without object; nor can we talk about object without subject. Thinking is always "about" something, an object. Thus, thinking is a continuum between subject and object.

The time has come to discard "subject" and "object" as terminology and create a term that shows the interconnectedness of subject and object. This new term contains both of the previous terms: Sobject.

I am no longer a subject for whom objects exist. I am being whose being is essentially tied to objects.

This appears to be a small point. It is not. I can say, for example, that thinking and action are not loose and separate, but interconnected. Thinking is not way over here, in this compartment, separated from another compartment, called action. Sobjects are always relating to and acting on objects. Objects always act on subjects.

5. Teaching and Learning: Teaching and learning is not a relationship between the spontaneous and the receptive.

What if human beings are both spontaneous and receptive beings? Does that affect the teaching-learning relationship?

The traditional student-teacher relationship is cast in the traditional subject-object dichotomy. Someone teaches and another learns. Someone is active, the other passive or receptive.

But we can re-examine this relationship in another way.

Say Jack tells Jill about the dangers of falling down hills and Jill is ignorant of this subject. Jill is not purely learning what Jack has to say about falling down hills, but is spontaneously organizing the material according to her particular social-historical world. She is not merely a receptacle to be filled up with information, but a being who possesses spontaneity. She is Sobject. Jack is not merely a classical Subject or pure spontaneity. If Jack wants Jill to learn what he is teaching her, he must be receptive to her questions, which teach him how to convey the information to her.

If the loving or caring relationship means we meet as equals, this suggests that Jill is not a purely repository waiting to be filled by Jack's knowledge and dominated by it. Rather, both are spontaneous and receptive. Jill is receptive to what Jack has to teach her, but never reduced to an object. For Jack, Jill is a being capable of her own spontaneity. She is capable of being a teacher.

6. Possibility: The "impossible" is an
ideological tool used to conceal possibilities.

Everything is thrown into question. That much has been established. No situation ever appears to us as finalized. Everything is open to change. This means that everything is possibility. Only one impossibility exists: That the possible is impossible with respect to the logically inconceivable. The world presents itself as a possibility to us. It presents itself as open to change.

A pedagogy of dynamism shows our lives open to possibility and as possibility. Possibility can happen to us, or we can be the ones who create possibility

Those lacking faith in their own creativity or in the creativity of others and who term radical social change as "impossible" are burdened by heavy sense of fatalism. The "impossible" also comes from the lips of those who want to conceal possibilities from those they oppress.

7. Possibility and the Invisible: The invisible is possible
(for all my friends who believe in God, the soul, and that paraphernalia)

Anything is possible.

This means that no possibility must be undermined. Possibilities that are not empirically verifiable in the traditional empirical way must not be marginalized or lampooned.

The existence of God and a soul, for example, are possibilities that human beings have conceived. Are we to consider them aberrations to a pedagogy of dynamism? Are they to be excluded?

If a pedagogy of dynamism discloses possibilities, then why should we rule out some possibilities and include others? The nature of belief is twofold. But beliefs crumble into disbeliefs. From disbeliefs or doubts beliefs arise.

A radical pedagogy should not be limited to a simple empiricist metaphysics. A radical pedagogy of dynamism reflects possibility. If we take possibility seriously, then our metaphysics must reflect all possibilities, even those that are invisible to us.

I hope you don't consider this to be false generosity on my part.

8. Rooting and Uprooting: The nature of self-consciousness is rooting and uprooting.

Our beliefs are also disbeliefs. Our disbeliefs are beliefs.

What does this suggest about human beings? I would like to put it in the following way: We are beings who continually root and uproot ourselves. Our beliefs root us, but are uprooted by our doubts. Our doubts uproot us, but we are also rooted by our beliefs. We may want to call human beings believing-disbelievers or unbelieving-believers. We want to root ourselves completely, but cannot. We want to uproot ourselves completely, but we cannot.

A radical pedagogy of dynamism never culminates in pure faith if by pure faith we mean an unquestioning attitude toward things. Nor can it encourage pure skepticism in which nothing is believed. I do not want to say that faith vacillates and becomes skepticism and that skepticism dissipates and becomes faith. Such a pedagogy sees faith and skepticism as part of an organic whole.

9. Inert Ideas and Sobjectivism: Sobjects are contrary to inert ideas.

Inert ideas can be viewed in the following ways:

(1) They can be viewed as old, tired ideas that have little significance to students.

(2) They can be deemed the result of students being passive recipients instead of imaginative integrators of ideas.

(3) They can be seen as cultivated by an inert presentation of ideas via monologue instead of via dynamic dialogue.

(4) They can be seen as disparate, compartmentalized ideas that remain isolated from one another instead of interrelated ideas that become dynamic in their constant "playing off" one another.

(5) They can be understood as arising from the traditional teacher-student hierarchy, in which teachers are oracles who own knowledge while students are vessels to be filled with knowledge they do not own.

(6) They are fostered by aesthetic respect, a superficial respect limited to rules, regulations, titles, and the like.

(7) They are the result of isolating facts from and elevating them over values.

When we meet others and others meet us as Sobjects, ideas become dynamic. Dynamic ideas of subjects (teachers) no longer become inert when deposited in objects (students). In relationships between Sobjects, all are spontaneous and receptive. I call such a relationship dialogue. Dialogue is dynamic not only because we and others spontaneously create ideas, but also because we and others are receptive to ideas. Being receptive to the ideas of others becomes the way in which our spontaneity is elicited.

10. Value-Laden Existence: Values are the bare essentials.

We are now in the so-called Information Age. We can go down the Information Superhighway and find virtually any fact we need. The one fact missing from the Information Superhighway is that no fact has meaning without value.

For human beings, everything is value-laden. On the most simple level, this means that we are attracted to or repulsed by things that we perceive. Attractiveness to things corresponds to our likes and our loves. Repulsion from things corresponds to our dislikes and hates. When something attracts us, we say that it is valuable to us. When something repulses us, we say that it is not valuable to us. We are attracted to beautiful things or ideals; we are repulsed by ugly things or anti-ideals.

Value is not limited to the level of primitive feeling. We can reflect on value. In a pedagogy of dynamism, reflection of value is of paramount importance. We must know which values we consider to be the guiding values of our lives. For example, Freire obviously believes that dehumanization is a negative value and the greatest evil and that humanization is positive value and the greatest good. Freire claims our ontological vocation to become more and more human. But this only describes our ontological vocation and excludes the underlying value judgment that humanization is the good, dehumanization the evil. Is there a separation between "This is what is" and "This is what is valuable"?

We immediately evaluate facts. We cannot avoid *evaluation*. The meaning of any fact is not exhausted until we *evaluate* that fact.

It is not enough for Freire to say that the ontological vocation of human beings is freedom. Freedom must be evaluated as a value, the supreme value, if we are going to act and commit ourselves. Commitment is not possible unless there are values to which we are committed. We are committed to cleaning up the environment because we are conservationists or preservationists. Either we value the earth for ourselves or value the earth for its own sake. Either we value human beings for themselves or we value them for our own sakes. The value judgment we accord to freedom will provide the framework for our commitment to freedom.

We are not committed to facts. We are not committed to "The sky is blue," or "Water is composed of hydrogen and oxygen," or "The universe is expanding." We are committed only to the value of those facts. Valuing a blue sky over smoggy sky; valuing clean water to dirty water; appraising our place in the universe and then valuing or disvaluing it ("Wow, we're part of the eternally changing cosmos" or "Damn, we're just dust in the wind and don't really matter").

In a radical pedagogy of dynamism, we must assess values in order to see through ideological contradictions. For example, if a society values equality, then why does an underclass exist? If a society values liberty, then why is freedom of speech curtailed? If a society values self-determination, why is it constantly invading other countries?

Facts and values walk hand in hand. The following chart features sixteen pairs of primitive concepts. The relationship between each pair is one of opposition.

Controllable	Uncontrollable
Commonality	Difference
Permanence	Process
One	Many
Receptivity	Spontaneity
Reduction	Irreduction
Simplicity	Complexity
Clarity	Ambiguity
Conformity	Resistance
Inertia	Dynamism
Order	Chaos
Belief	Doubt
Predictability	Unpredictability
Eternity	Ephemerality
Design	Accident
Efficiency	Inefficiency

Negotiations take place between the pairs of primitives as well as between different pairs determines the values of facts. In negotiations between clarity and ambiguity, I may value clarity. I ask why. I discover that the clearer, the more controllable. The more controllable, the more predictable. And the more predictable, the more efficient.

Let us say that I value dynamism over inertia. Specific valuations underlie or complement this valuation. Can I value dynamism without valuing the complex over the simple? Can I value dynamism without valuing the irreducible over the reducible? Can I value dynamism without valuing ambiguity over clarity? Can I value dynamism without valuing unpredictability over predictability? I value dynamism on the basis of affirming the related values of complexity, irreducibility, ambiguity, and unpredictability.

Let us say I value design over accident. The values of predictability, belief, order, clarity, and reduction are complementary values. The values of unpredictability, doubt, and chaos are uncomplementary values. Whatever has a design is far more predictable than something that lacks design. Whatever is predictable is far more conducive to belief than to doubt.

Can we hold absolute values and still remain true to our radical pedagogy of dynamism? Can we avoid sectarianism, dogmatism, and sophistry if we hold absolute values? As long we do not hold absolute values as icons and unassailable and fail to see that we could be wrong about our assertion that they are absolute values, then we can remain true to our radical pedagogy of dynamism.

11. Reformers Are Deformers:
Something is not always better than nothing.

Beware of strangers bearing gifts.

The gifts of reformers are tasty to the good-hearted and well-intentioned, but ultimately retard the oppressed.

The gifts of reformers are tasty. This is because they offer us superficial change and not deep change. They appeal to our humanitarian instincts. They appeal to our goodness and our benevolence. But they also appeal to us because they do not produce much inconvenience. Most anybody can become a reformer.

Reform is not aimed at the core of the system, but only its most superficial elements. Reform does not endanger the fundamental institutions of a society. Reform keeps us within the same system.

Reform maintains the status quo more than any conservatism does. This is because reform is fraudulent. It gives the impression we are addressing root problems when we are not. It gives the impression we are progressing when we are retrogressing or staying in the same place.

Reform gives us false hope that things are really changing for the better. Nothing is really changing. The only thing changing is our perception that things are changing. Reform never pushes toward core issues.

Reform and radicalism are not the same. Reform is always sectarian. Reform means to work within a safeguarded framework. It means to work within the system. By its nature, reform excludes possibilities, in particular, that the present system is failing and must be supplanted.

Radicalism leaves open the possibility that the present system must be replaced. Radicalism is the true manifestation of a pedagogy of dynamism. A pedagogy of dynamism points to all possibilities.

In the final analysis, reform is half-hearted, indecent, and ineffective. It promises more than it can ever deliver. Reform can be welcomed as a way to placate dissenting factions of an organization. Measures of reform are at best moderate and do nothing to endanger the core of power. Reform leaves the core of power intact. Reform is characterized by false generosity. It throws crumbs and praises itself for throwing crumbs, believing that these crumbs are banquets.

Reform is the epitome of hypocrisy and cowardice. Reformers reform only what does not endanger the status quo. They reform only what truly does not matter and what does not endanger them personally. In one small and insignificant area they reform. The larger and more important area, they do not touch.

Radical pedagogy does not welcome reform.

12. The Pledge of Allegiance: Learning is learning to rebel.

Pedagogy must address the following question from early on: What is a good society?

To answer that question we must ask others.

What are the fundamental needs of human beings?

How does a good society meet those needs?

Who should be involved in the dialogue to determine those needs?

Radical pedagogy points to Thomas Jefferson's statement in the Declaration of Independence, which reads: "That whenever any Form of Government becomes destructive of these ends [Life, Liberty, and the pursuit of Happiness], it is the Right of the People to alter or to abolish it, and to institute new government." Incidentally, this is the same point of departure for Black Panther ideology. Radical pedagogy encourages constant reflection on the nature of the good life and how institutions serve to bring about the good life.

Critiques of the government means critique of fundamental ideological assumptions and actions that reflect those ideological assumptions. For example, if a country says that it values democracy and promotes democracy throughout the world, then both that ideological assumption and its enactment concerning policies must be addressed.

Reformers, even if they bother to quote Jefferson, will say that his words do not apply to the present state of affairs. Ours is a different world, they say. But Jefferson's apply not only to this era, but to all eras. Political and social awareness means addressing our government's ideology and policies.

If our government says it is a democracy, for example, then we should attempt to understand whether the people have a voice or whether an elite actually is running the country under that guise. This should be a priority of schooling and constitute "social studies." If the foreign policy of our country is to bring democracy, freedom, and the free market to other parts of the world, we must evaluate whether our deeds in those place correspond to those lofty ideals. That is primary. We can never have blind faith that the government will do the right thing.

Instead of saying the pledge of allegiance to the flag each morning, students should say a pledge of allegiance to eliminate all oppression and help all realize the good life.

13. Faith and Trust: The greatest faith in myself and others is in our creative powers and our ability to think.

A pedagogy of dynamism does not invalidate trust and faith. It merely redefines them. Trust and faith are imperative to a pedagogy of dynamism. Without them, we are completely uprooted.

In accordance with my earlier definition of self-consciousness, trust and faith are never immediate. Trust and faith are never blind. Trust and faith, as forms of belief, give rise to distrust and faithlessness. But because they give rise to distrust and faithlessness does not mean that distrust and faithlessness are permanent either.

A pedagogy of dynamism does not consist of naive trust or faith in another person. A naive or doubt-free faith is not possible, according to our description of self-consciousness. We can only "hang on to" faith or trust, as we hang on to the fingers of a person whom we are saving from falling into a precipice.

Faith and trust are perilous and always slipping away. But we can have faith and trust in others. A radical pedagogy has faith and trust in creativity.

Faith and trust in our creativity means that nothing is beyond redemption. No matter what happens to us, no matter what others do to us, we can recreate the world.

Trust and faith in creativity rests at the center of a pedagogy of dynamism. To endorse a pedagogy of dynamism without also endorsing a pedagogy of creativity is like sending a child out into a blizzard without any clothes. Creativity is the way we regenerate our world. We can endure and even flourish in doubt if we know that in the end we are the creators of our world.

Trust and faith in creativity circumscribe other forms of trust and faith. When betrayed by others, especially on a repeated basis, people have a hard time trusting others. They are wary of being hurt again. The faith and trust in creativity makes us view the world in this way: No matter what happens, I can create a solution for the problem—everything is salvageable.

Faith and trust in my creativity allow me to face and not flee from the ambiguous. When no solutions are immediately available, we face ambiguity. The faith to face ambiguous situations courageously presupposes faith and trust in my creative powers (creatively defining the world) lays the groundwork for my trust in others and in my existence in general. My faith and trust in my creative powers undermines my fear of existence.

When I affirm my creativity, I affirm the faith that I can shape the world. The more I trust and have faith in myself, the more trust and faith I have in others, I would say. Those who see themselves as devoid of creativity play a purely reactive game with the world. The world acts on them and they feel helpless. Faith and trust in creativity suggest taking an active part in the world. It means faith in empowerment

Courage comes easily to me when I trust in my creative powers. Everybody and everything is a possibility, not a threat, for me. Cowardice comes easily to me when I distrust my creative powers. Believing that I lack creativity, everything and everybody pose a threat to me.

I am not referring to the creativity of renowned geniuses. I am referring to the creative powers that human beings possess to mold and shape the world, for example, with respect to our every-day decisions and our belief systems.

14. Commitment: I am committed to others only to the extent that I trust them to be creative and therefore self-determining beings.

Our commitment to others begins in the initial stage of fellow-feeling, or caring. Commitment is not simply an intellectual exercise divorced from feeling. As Martin Luther King, Jr. says, we must not only be tough-minded but also tender-hearted.[2] Heart and intellect, not intellect alone, provide the basis for commitment. When we are committed to others, it is as if we drawn toward them to help them flourish or to mitigate or eliminate their pain. Others are regarded unconditionally. Any deterioration from unconditional value reduces others to things.

Commitment arises in our common contact with other people. From this initial humanizing contact arise trust or faith, hope, and solidarity.

At the outset, fellow-feeling bonds us to others. But fellow-feeling alone cannot produce commitment. Not only must we care for others, but we must believe that they are creative enough to make their way in the world, make their decisions, and fashion their lives. Fellow-feeling without this faith in the creativity of others devolves into paternalism.

Fellow-feeling supplies the initial interest in the affairs of others and provides the basis for our assessment of their unconditional worth. But commitment to others is more complex than mere fellow-feeling or caring. We must believe that others can interpret the world. Interpretation consists of mediating between various perspectives and from them arriving at a decision concerning the world. Our faith is in others being able to "negotiate" themselves.

Belief in the creativity of others provides the groundwork for hope. Hope is buoyed if we believe in the creativity of others. If we do not believe that others can create, then what are we left with? Can we be hopeful if we believe that the people, the majority of people, are incompetents? When we believe others are competent, are creative in the sense to which we have been speaking, then hope arises. We realize that the collective community of creators can change the world. Once we have faith in a collective community of creators, we then feel solidarity with others as co-creators of the world. At this stage, our commitment is full.

All of this is fine, you say, but what about the nature of thinking as you have described it: How does that affect commitment? Thinking always transcends itself. Wouldn't it thereby transcend commitments, going from one to another, never settling on one? How can we be committed if our commitments are always changing?

This brings us to the question of commitment to unchanging values, no matter how our thinking changes. We can only be committed to those values that we have reflected on for a long time and we consider to be verities. Fellow-feeling with others suggests that others must be treated as unconditional beings and can provide the basis for the principle of the humanization of others. Once we arrive at what we believe to be the truth, then our commitment can be deeper. Shallow commitments are based on principles or values that have not been thoroughly evaluated.

In a radical pedagogy of dynamism, can we ever be uncommitted? Being uncommitted suggests not binding ourselves to a behavior, to be disengaged. But nobody can be disengaged, if by disengagement we mean the pure posture of doubting. Every doubt dovetails into a belief. We are half-doubters and half-believers. We are always at least half-engaged, whether we like it or not. We are always at least half-disengaged, whether we like it or not.

15. Innatism: Trust in the innate abilities of others should be tinctured by the recognition of oppressive forces forces that prevent the emergence of these innate qualities.

A radical pedagogy arises around the idea of faith in the creativity of others. It does not take the view that others are empty vessels to be filled up by knowledge. The banking concept offers a pretext to program others and easily conforms to vertical or hierarchical schooling. It offers an excuse for paternalism and control of others. The contrary to the "empty mind" is not acceptable to a pedagogy of radical pedagogy either. If we say that human beings possess innate gifts and that outside forces do nothing to prevent their emergence, then we can adhere to Social Darwinism and do nothing to change oppressive conditions. We have heard this pernicious view explained as "Some birds are born black and others are born white," which means: "Some people are born intelligent, others stupid, and we can't do anything to alter their intelligence."

The view to which a radical pedagogy of dynamism is committed is this: People possess innate qualities that are prevented from emerging because of oppressive elements around them. The project of schooling is to identify and eliminate those forces that prevent the emergence of our potentialities.

16. Ambiguity: Ambiguity is not a disease to be wiped out, but a cure for the toxin of narrow clarity.

In *On Education and Values: In Praise of Pariahs and Nomads*, Conrad P. Pritscher and I make a case for the importance of ambiguity.[3] We contend that chaos is necessary for thinking to occur at all. Thinking occurs only when we are faced with contradictions, paradoxes, and ambiguity. This may be seen as "chaos" within our thinking. It may appear to be anarchy. But our view is that thinking only emerges when we emerge from the chaos and clarify the world. This does not mean that the goal of thinking is increasing clarification.

The truth is is that things that become overly clarified do not cultivate thinking at all. This is because the contradictions, paradoxes, conundrums, and ambiguities in general are the result of interpreting the world. If we are intellectually promiscuous, as all thinking should be, then there is a continuous integration and negotiation among different perspectives. Integrating perspectives is the nature of interpretation, as I have defined it. Discovering the deep contradictions between differing perspectives and attempting to resolve them represents the essence of thinking. Narrow clarity is not intellectually promiscuous. Narrow clarity will not allow for a wide range of options because that would complicate matters and introduce ambiguity. Everything can be simple if we eliminate the contradictions and thus the ambiguities. Issues can be quickly settled. Ambiguity is often run out of the classroom like the unwelcome visitor who is run out of town.

Religions often possess a narrow clarity. Contradictions are prevented from arising. This is similar to what Noam Chomsky describes in *Necessary Illusions*[4] Chomsky's propaganda model stipulates that the elites who control the flow of information allow a limited degree or narrow range of opinion. Contradictions arise and then readers have to negotiate or interpret in order to discover the truth. Narrow clarity is one of the portents of propaganda.

Propaganda cannot stand contradictions. Contradictions serve to invalidate the flimsy claims propaganda. Contradictions serve to further thinking, not stifle it. Contradictions undermine authority. Authorities often rule in clarity. What they say is clear and simple and concise. Everything is spelled out. In that way, questions do not arise. Contradictions must be banished. So must those whose questions serve to introduce contradictions.

This is not to say that thinking is finished by introducing contradiction or ambiguity. Thinking only begins in the midst of contradiction or ambiguity. As soon as a set of contradictions is resolved, then others arise.

Ambiguity can never be driven out of thinking. The nature of thinking is to transcend. The continual transforming of thinking necessarily makes thinking ambiguous. People can deny ambiguity. They can try to drive a stake through its heart as if it were a vampire. But it cannot die until we ourselves die.

Some people are not ready for ambiguity, you may argue. They would drown. It would be like throwing them into a pool without a swimming lesson. But people need not be taught to think. They need only be led to see the nature of their self-consciousness. Then thinking becomes easy.

If we can lead people to see themselves, then we can cultivate thinking. It is not a matter of throwing them in the pool and hoping that they will swim, but a matter of holding up a mirror and letting them see themselves.

17. Sharing History: History is not private property.

The highest form of solidarity with others is believing that they possess the creativity to shape their lives. Commitment to such solidarity encourages us to share the making of history with others. Not only are we co-cognizers and recreators of knowledge, we are also co-owners of history.

A close relationship exists between the two. Sharing the naming of the world with others implies that the world is co-owned. An element of this sharing is the sharing of history. We historicize the world by naming it.

History is not something that others create for us and then we follow. We are all part of the process, and we are all responsible for historicizing the world.

History is not private property. It is co-produced and thus co-owned by all. In a radical pedagogy of dynamism, history is not something that happens to people. People create history. The supposition of freedom entails that the world can be shaped and formed by us.

When we view history seen as something that happens to us, or something out of our control, or something inert, then we are alienated from our creativity. We cannot call ourselves "self-determining" being if history remains something that others create. History becomes "living history" only to the extent that we take responsibility for its production.

18. Being Less than Generous:
Cut off the helping hands of false generosity.

If we believe others to be capable of self-determination, we believe that they can make their own decisions. We believe that they possess the creative means to survive and flourish.

This being the case, the supposition of self-determination excludes all forms of paternalism. Paternalism implies lack of faith in another's creativity. Lack of faith in another's creativity lays the groundwork for paternalism.

Lack of faith in another's creativity lays the groundwork for an inert pedagogy. The assumption is made that the uncreative can only grasp what is clear and simple. The clear and the simple is most always the unambiguous. And the unambiguous is usually the inert.

Thus, a relationship exists between Whitehead's inert ideas, creativity, and self-determination. Inert ideas in education suggest Freire's banking concept of education. This assumes that students lack creativity and must be force-fed (horrible medicine jammed down the throat by a callous doctor) or spoon-fed (delicious medicine administered by the kind Mary Poppins). Whether force-fed or spoon-fed, it still amounts to paternalism. It shows no faith in the ability of others to make decisions.

Inert ideas vanish to the extent that self-determination and creativity are honored. Ideas that were once inert become vitalized to the extent that people are allowed to inject them with their own vitality. The best way to prevent ideas from becoming inert is to remove paternalism from the classroom and to affirm creativity and self-determination.

Another important relationship exists: the relationship between self-determination, creativity, and ambiguity. The less paternalistic an environment, the more ambiguity. The more ambiguity, the more openness for interpretation on the part of students. Inert ideas arise from paternalistic teaching styles. Paternalism sets limits instead of allowing students to create limits. Paternalism is always overarching. The "helping hand" of paternalism turns out to be vice-like grip meant to cut off the circulation of the hands that are extended to it.

19. Integrating toward Truth:
The more we interpret, the more we negotiate.

We must allow the our views to be formed from negotiations. Non-paternalistic classrooms allow for negotiation and integration. Affirmation of interpretation necessarily entails the affirmation of creativity. If creativity and self-determination go hand-in-hand, then interpretation must also go in the same hand.

In the banking concept of education, students merely mimic their teachers. Some forms of what is commonly called "understanding" are counterfeits for imitation. The word "understanding" literally means to stand under. The most effective way of "standing under" is to interpret.

"Interpretation" has often been used in the negative sense. Sometimes interpretation is contrasted with objectivity. The objective is the true and then we have various interpretations of the true. "You have your interpretation and I have mine" is also a frequent way "interpret" is understood. In this sense, only different perspectives exist and one is as good or as bad as another.

I see "interpretations" in a far different way. Let us begin by looking at the root of "interpret." We can trace "interpret" back to the Latin *interpres,* which means negotiator or explainer. Interpretation involves some form of negotiation or integration of perspectives. How does negotiation figure into pedagogy? Truth emerges in negotiation. Ultimately, truth emerges in negotiation of different positions. Dialogue is essential to interpretation because dialogue brings out disparate positions. We form our views on issues by negotiating between different perspectives. Most of the times these negotiations are complex. We interpret to the extent that there are negotiations between various perspectives.

We "stand under" issues to the extent that we interpret them. Interpretation, in my sense, does not mean bringing a specific viewpoint to an issue. It means a continuous negotiation between perspectives. From this negotiation, our viewpoints are formed.

Interpretation, then, is not simply a viewpoint imposed on the world. It represents a creative negotiation among viewpoints. Negotiation is always one of ambiguity and contradiction because negotiations involve contradictory positions. Reconciling these contradictions and in the process creating different contradictions is the end result of negotiation.

No issue is ever permanently negotiated. Negotiation itself is continuous. We can never say: "Negotiations are at an end." We can only say: "At this point, we have reached a temporary settlement." This settlement is always temporary because self-consciousness naturally transcends the settlement and pushes toward other disputes and settlements.

Thus the more we interpret, the more we negotiate and integrate toward truth.

20. Philosophy and Religion: Writing the birth announcement for philosophy means writing the obituary for religion.

A pedagogy of dynamism can accommodate only philosophy. It cannot accommodate religion. What I mean by religion and philosophy are different from what most people think. By religion, I don't mean Judaism, Christianity, or Satanism. I mean a fundamental attitude toward the world in which first principles are not challenged. In a radical pedagogy everything is challenged. The most cherished principles are subject to scrutiny. Religion, then, is the antipode of philosophy and at best is reform.

A pedagogy of dynamism means the continuous rethinking of our viewpoint. Religion never descends beyond the superficial to peer at what is beneath. Its first principles are never in jeopardy. Philosophy means that first principles are thrown into jeopardy.

This is not to say that philosophy does not have first principles. It only means that philosophy is wed to first principles only until they can be replaced. While religion is married only once to first principles, philosophy may be wed many times to first principles

Philosophy is never monogamous. Philosophy is promiscuous. Many persons find it hard to be monogamous. Promiscuity is easier. The opposite is true for philosophy. Philosophy must maintain its promiscuity and guard against monogamy.

The monogamous philosopher is: a Theologian!

21. Philosophy as Intellectual Promiscuity: Philosophy is always promiscuous.

A pedagogy of dynamism is a pedagogy of intellectual promiscuity. This means that we never satisfy ourselves on just one perspective. We are continually searching for new perspectives to complement our own. We desire intercourse everywhere and anywhere with other perspectives. We do not remain intellectual virgins.

Intellectual virgins never allow themselves to be shaped by other perspectives. Intellectual virgins do not want to negotiate with others. Negotiation is not part of the repertoire of the intellectual virgin. Negotiation is only possible for the intellectually promiscuous.

Philosophy is nothing more than intellectual promiscuity. No one who is a philosopher is a virgin. Philosophy laughs at intellectual virgins, who are the victims of their innocence and ignorance.

A pedagogy of dynamism is promiscuous. Hence, a pedagogy of dynamism is characterized by philosophy. Philosophy is the name we give for our pedagogy of dynamism.

22. Respect: Radical pedagogy accepts only a certain forms of respect.

Granted, too little respect exists in the world. But this does not mean that what some people mean by respect would be conducive to radical pedagogy. Radical pedagogy cannot accommodate respect, if respect is charged with fear.

Fear has no place in a horizontal classroom. Respect of this sort is used when the traditional teacher-student relationship is enforced. It helps maintain teachers as the sole authority and stifles dialogue. It prevents challenges to authority.

Another form of respect amounts to reverence. But whenever something is reverenced, it cannot be questioned. The divine cannot be challenged. Nothing is reverenced in a pedagogy of dynamism.

The respect that I wish to see in the dialogical classroom is an equal respect for others as persons. This means that no person can be reduced to the status of a thing. But this does not mean that anyone or anyone's view is reverenced. It suggests that truth must be sought, even if people are offended by truth.

I am not arguing for arguing for disrespect in the classroom. Challenging the reverenced is not disrespect. Discussing the obscene is not disrespect. Challenging anybody about anything is not disrespect.

We need to look at disrespect in another fashion. The greatest source of disrespect is paternalism. Paternalism implies a distrust of the competence of others. It suggests that others are not creative and thus lack self-determination. Respect for others entails the trust in the competence, creativity, and the self-determination of others.

What is respect for difference? Respect for difference is respect for others to live and shape their lives as they feel fit. Respect for difference presupposes intellectual promiscuity, because in order to respect difference, we must be able to identify and understand it as difference, identify the particular difference. Respect for difference involves a fellow-feeling or act of caring in which I am moved to understand the other. Thus, respect for difference is not simply an abstract way of regarding difference. It is rooted in our relatedness to others.

Respect for difference is fostered by comprehending our changing or differing selves. Once we recognize and accept the alien or difference in ourselves, then we can more easily recognize and accept the alien in others.

23. Respect and Obscenity: Reserve respect for obscenity.

The obscene is whatever we believe to be taboo.

In traditional pedagogy, obscenity is rarely mentioned. It remains outside the realm of schooling. In a radical pedagogy, obscenity is respected. It is respected because obscenity is reserved for those topics that a society considers most loathsome.

The obscene is an essential subject matter for a radical pedagogy of dynamism. The obscene transcends the bounds of the proper and delves into the improper. The ugly, repressed truths of a society are closeted. A radical pedagogy of dynamism opens the closet door.

But these are precisely those themes that a pedagogy of dynamism must address. The so-called obscene (most notably, sex) cannot be excluded from inquiry. The only reason that the obscene is removed from inquiry is because of the reverence of reverence. Once we introduce too much reverence for reverence, then the obscene cannot come into play. The reverenced cannot be adulterated by the obscene. The obscene casts aspersions on the reverenced.

Without overarching reverence, obscenity can be discussed. Once we see the reverenced as obscene, then we must focus on the obscene. In the obscene, we will find our darkest, most troubling, and most repressed feelings and thoughts. Only through an examination of the obscene will we find ourselves.

Once we have addressed the obscene as our society sees it, we must find out whether this represents a sham or real obscenity. Let me take a case in point: sexuality. For many in the United States, sexuality still remains a taboo subject. But aren't there many more things more obscene than a penis or vagina? For example, dropping bombs on innocent people, as the United States did to Cambodians, may be considered obscene. Whatever is most obscene should match what we consider the be the most brutal things we can do to our beings. The fact that something is deemed "obscene" should not prevent discussion of it.

Pedagogy should not avoid obscene things for fear of disrespecting others. Some people might argue that it is disrespectful to discuss the obscene. Perhaps the opposing argument is more true: It is disrespectful not to include the obscene in discussion. The obscene, some argue, may make people uncomfortable. Comfort is what people most desire. Comfortable means: not discussing or challenging what diverges from my belief system. Comfort means: making schooling one big Lazy Boy Recliner. But in those recliners, we tend to fall asleep. A pedagogy of dynamism is uncomfortable. It prides itself on the discomfort it brings. Disrespect means creating an unchallenging pedagogy, characterized by sterilizing comfort. It means excluding the most extreme forms of discomfort (obscenity), which might cause undue anxiety.

Thus, encourage the study of obscene things. The more, the better. This will bring to light our identity of persons and our identity as a society. The obscene is what a society considers to be the profane. But the profane has a very interesting relationship with the profound. In fact, the profane is at times the profound. The profound must be distinguished from the trivial. The trivial is the constantly reiterated. The profound can become trivial when reiterated to death, becoming as Freire says, a verbalism. The profound shocks us from our common perceptions and sensibilities.

24. Triviality: Triviality is the bastion of inert ideas.

The subject matter does not matter in education any more. The only thing that matter is appearing to know. Actual knowing is for the fools who actually believe that knowing is important. Teaching becomes PYOA (Protect Your Own Ass). Don't be controversial: you might get sued. Don't be obscene: that wouldn't be appropriate and you might get sued. Water down everything to the least common denominator: you might not get sued. Don't make interconnections between your discipline and others. Focus on grades and the penalties and rewards for not realizing those grades. Refuse to conduct thought-experiments in which you don't have the solution to a problem. Don't be profound: you may get sued.

Congratulations, professor, you have just trivialized schooling. You have deflected attention from the substance of learning (dialogue) to trivialities. You have trivialized learning by not showing the intrinsic relationship between the theoretical and the practical. You have trivialized learning by not showing the relationship between the type of education and the type of society. You have trivialized education by thoughting rather than thinking. What you call dialogue, I call a contest of triviality. Your dialogue never goes beyond mere name-calling and surface assertions. Your depoliticized classroom is a breeding ground for the apolitical citizen. Contradictions of the nature of the society are left unchallenged in any significant way.

Triviality is the king of the classroom. Students know only trivia. They are unable to transcend trivia and grasp interconnections and cultivate a holistic attitude. The profound always grasps interconnections. Profundity sees more than things: it sees between things. Trivia is about things. Profundity is creating and grasping connections between things. The gap between facts that is the place for profundity. Nowhere else.

Schooling in the United States is a trivial and not a profound pursuit. Schooling is for the purpose of becoming a cog in the wheel. Schooling rarely challenges the cog or the wheel. Schooling purveys but does not challenge ideology. Questions such as "Who am I?" and "What is a human being?" cannot be answered apart from understanding the ideology of a society. Take human nature. We must understand what our society's values are and understand how and why they affect our perceptions of human nature. It is in the best interests of someone who supports capitalism to say that human beings are inherently competitive and selfish. It furthers capitalist ideology and the power structure that the ideology supports.

The inoffensive is always the trivial. The inoffensive is the accepted canon. It cannot challenge. It is what everybody already knows. The offensive is not always trivial. The offensive pushes beyond the accepted canon. But because something is deemed offensive does exclude it from triviality. Offensiveness need not be profound. But it lends itself toward creating a gateway to the profound because profundity is often associated with taboo or offensive topics.

25. Thinking and Thought:
Only thinking is allowed; thought on your own.

A radical pedagogy sees thinking as a continuous process. It never ceases. Thought can never be allowed. For thought is thinking left on the counter without a lid and gone rotten. Thought is the past and is dead. Thinking is directed to the past and incorporates the past and the future with it.

Thinking is our interpretation of the world, if by interpretation we mean "negotiation." Reconciliation of varying perspectives is thinking. Thinking never swerves around contradictions. It seeks contradictions in order to reconcile them.

Thought rejects contradictions. For contradictions create ambiguity. Thought recoils from any becoming. Thought is set in stone. Thought recoils from doubt. It wants crystal clear certainty. It never negotiates and reaches out to negotiate and integrate, but reaches toward the paternalistic hand that will keep it as thought and not as thinking.

Thinking is not limited to a mental activity. Thinking in its most profound sense is the interrelationship of contemplation and action. This action I have called "negotiation." Thinking wants to become "enhanced" by other perspectives. Thought recoils from negotiation, believing negotiation will tarnish it.

26. The Neutron Bomb Analogy:
Making room for thinking means the exodus of all icons.

Icons are the reverenced.

Reverence has no place in thinking. The reverenced stifles thinking. What we revere we worship. And worship has no place in thinking. The reverenced must be forcibly removed for thinking to take place.

As a means to remove icons and reverence, I propose a neutron bomb approach to education. The neutron bomb destroys all life but leaves buildings intact. For government officials, it left intact what it deemed essential. My neutron bomb pedagogy rids us of what I believe to be inessential: icons. It leaves standing only what is essential: the dynamism of thinking and fellow-feeling.

A radical pedagogy is necessarily a neutron bomb approach to education. The foundation for icons is lacking in a pedagogy of becoming for two fundamental and interrelated reasons: (1) the reverenced can only emerge in thought, when the world is reduced to stasis, and (2) the reverenced can only emerge when the obscene is concealed.

Thinking, as I have described it, leaves no room for iconization. Icons are produced only when belief is not mixed with disbelief. If we understand thinking as both belief and disbelief, then icons are prevented from arising.

Why do icons arise if thinking is by nature dynamic? All icons are the result of a denial of thinking. All icons are the result of thought. In denying the dynamism of thinking, objects can be taken as reverenced. The reverenced cannot come under assault. The reverenced never can come into negotiation. The reverenced is removed from the world and mummified.

What remains without icons? Thinking and fellow-feeling: thinking, which inevitably runs ahead of itself, and fellow-feeling, which is our connectedness with others and in which values arise. The neutron bombs I propose leave intact thinking and fellow-feeling. It allows for the dynamism of thinking and our fundamental caring connectedness with others

27. Genuine and False Hope: The more creative, the more hopeful.

The world is transformable.

A situation can become this or that. Or I may transform a situation from this to that. In the first case, I look on the world in a passive way. In the second, I look on the world in an active way.

A passive regard for the discourages hope and forms the basis of hopelessness. The reason for this sense of hopelessness is our alienation from our creative powers. Believing that change is possible means two things: that the world is open to change and that I can bring change about in the world. If either of these elements is missing, then I will not believe that change is possible. If I believe the world is dynamic, but that a power other than myself initiates change, then my creative powers are neutralized. The same result occurs when I believe the world is closed to change, but that I have some kind of creative impulse.

Hope comes into being only when I believe that the world is open to change and that I am capable of changing it. Hope rides on the back of creativity and thus our self-determination. The more we believe in self-determination, the greater our hope. Self-determination rests on the supposition that I can change the world and that the world is open to change. I can determine my world. The discussion of self-determination cannot be left on the level of the individual and a narrowly conceived world. The discussion of self-determination must include social and political institutions. Unless these institutions are believed to be open to change, then full self-determination is not possible. Cultivating creativity on the personal basis, but not on the political basis, is not cultivating self-determination at all.

Cultivating creativity without the belief that the larger social framework is unable to be changed is to set up what I shall call "the creativity *cul-de-sac*." In the creativity *cul-de-sac*, creativity is fostered, but then fizzles when it hits the brick wall, the intractable and unreceptive social and political reality. The social and political world is largely unopen to my creative attempts to change it. Eventually, after much effort, I lose all my desire to create and become "receptive" only. Creativity then recoils back on me and like an anaconda wraps itself around me and squeezes the life out of me.

False hope quickly turns into fatalistic attitudes, apathy, and eventually despair. Faith in my creativity alone does not circumvent this problem. I must have faith in others to bring about a world in which the full range of self-determination is possible. Only in conjunction with others can social institutions be created and sustained to allow room for self-determination.

Thus, my faith is not simply in my creativity, but in the creativity of all people. Only through the collective creativity of all people will self-determination be possible. Hence, that all people are free (self-determining and thus creative beings) is a prerequisite for my being free.

28. Alienation:
Alienation is not a fact of life, but a fact of oppression.

Alienation has been a fundamental theme of Western thought. For Christianity, we have been alienated since the fall from Eden and the alienation will continue until the return of the Christ. For Hegel, humanity's alienation ceases when the subject-object relationship is understood in the final phase, which he calls Absolute Knowing. In *Philosophical and Economic Manuscripts of 1844*, Marx enunciates four fundamental forms of alienation: (1) alienation from the product we create; (2) alienation from our activity; (3) alienation from our human essence; and (4) alienation from other people.[5] In *Being and Nothingness*, Jean-Paul Sartre describes the basic project of human beings as an alienation beyond any redemption. The nature of self-consciousness is that human beings are what they are not and are not what they are. This gap or hole in being can never be repaired. We are haunted by the ideal, but can never attain it.

The view of Hegel and Marx view is that history is a battle ground for alienation that will by necessity disappear at the end of the process. History is inherently aimed toward the elimination of alienation. Sartre's view is that history has nothing to do with alienation. Alienation is a fact of human reality. No matter the society, alienation cannot be removed.

Where history is going and when and where it will culminate in de-alienation is beyond the scope of human knowledge. I take the view that the future can be created by human beings. When we say that history will take this or that course regardless of what we do, this amounts to alienation from history.

If a future is going to occur, no matter what we do, then we are alienated from bringing it about ourselves. If the future is our creation, then we are not alienated from it. We rob ourselves of our freedom by believing that anything is inevitable. Nothing is inevitable from the human standpoint.

A radical pedagogy dynamism sees the future as realizable by those in the present. We have the freedom to bring about this or that future.

Sartre depicts human beings as Sisyphus in Hades. Like Sisyphus, our desires can never be fulfilled. We push the rock up the hill only to have it come back down on us. Our unhappy consciousness is the result of wanting to be whole and full (without consciousness), yet at the same time possessing self-consciousness. In other words, we want to be God.

Satisfaction is not possible. No matter what we achieve or do, something is always lacking. We can never rid ourselves of this lacking. This is because we are, by the nature of our self-consciousness, lacking. We are beings who lack.

I wish to address Sartre's understanding of lack by first addressing degrees of lacking. For Sartre, human reality is cast in either-or terms: Either we possess complete satisfaction and are de-alieneated or we lack complete satisfaction and are alienated. We are anguished beings because we can never reach the state of perfection. But what if we cast the problem in another way, in terms of degrees of alienation? Should we look at "lacking" in terms of the degree to which something is lacking?

No matter how much someone loves us, it can never be enough. No matter how much money or how many possessions we have, it can never be enough. A standard of perfection always stares us in the face and reminds us of our imperfection. But we can recognize degrees of approaching this standard of perfection. We can realize that even though we will never be loved as we want to be loved (in an ideal way), we can differentiate degrees of being loved. The way one person loves us is closer to the ideal than the way another person loves us. We perceive the difference in the lacking. If even vaguely in our minds we differentiate between degrees of lacking, then our anguish fades. We realize that we have it better now than we did in the past. Or we realize that we can have it better in the future than we have it now. We can be feel joy in now being loved now more than we were in the past or look forward to being loved in the future more than we are now. In being able to progress toward the ideal, we gradually de-alienate ourselves. In believing that we have the creativity to progress toward the ideal, we gradually dealienate ourselves.

Perhaps Sartre is culpable of setting up an "alienation paradox." This is similar to what is called the "happiness paradox." The happiness paradox states that the more people try to become happy, the more unhappy they grow. Happiness has been turned into a thing that really cannot be attained. In this case, happiness has to be captured, as if it were in a box. The same thing holds true for alienation, as Sartre presents it. Those who are seeking this static thing called "de-alienation" are doomed to fail. De-alienation can be accomplished by recognizing the chase, not what is captured, as the end. We are more or less alienated to the degree that we approach the ideal. We gain satisfaction by approaching the ideal. We experience more or less anguish to the extent we approach the ideal.

Alienation, as Sartre understands it, is alienation from our true nature of becomers. We are always cutting and honing the stone. The stone is under constant revision and repair. Understanding ourselves as beings in becoming is to create joy in the dynamism of existence. We are not capable of absolute joy, any more than we are of absolute knowing. Those goals, though unattainable, are approachable. By defining a standard, even an unattainable one, we can gauge to what degree we approach those ideals. We may never reach the other end of the pool. But we can determine how far we have gone across the swimming pool.

In a radical pedagogy of dynamism, the ideal is that of a world in which all people will be self-determining beings. The degree to which the world is moving toward that direction will determine the level of anguish. Though the ideal will never be realized, this does not mean that we are totally alienated. What is total alienation anyway? Total alienation is the anti-ideal as compared to total de-alienation. If we compare ourselves with complete de-alienation, then do we also compare ourselves with complete alienation? If we can conceive of the greatest goodness (God), can we also think of the greatest lack of goodness or evil (Satan)? We know we are not God; that would not be possible. We also know we are not Satan; that, too, would be impossible. Our anguish in not being perfectly good is mitigated by our happiness of not being perfectly evil. Analogously, our anguish at not being totally de-alienated is offset by our happiness of not being totally alienated. Plato said that human beings are between knowledge and ignorance. We may feel anguish in not knowing everything, but we have joy in knowing some things and in knowing at least that we do not know.

Anguish may arise for not being the totality, but joy may arise from being more than nothing. For Sartre, we as human beings are anguish because we lack the ideal. Don't we also lack the opposite, the anti-ideal, which is no less realizable than the ideal? We cannot become purely dissatisfied any more than we can become purely satisfied. Being the lack of dissatisfaction brings us joy.

My radical pedagogy refuses to allow alienation, as Sartre and others define it, to become an ideology. When we accept alienation as a fact of life, then we find nothing towards which to strive. We will always hate ourselves and hate others and no real progress can be made. The world will always have rich, will always have poor, will always have oppressors and those who are oppressed. The best we can do is wallow around in this shit that is humanity, waiting anxiously for the day that the whole human race becomes extinct.

We can never be at one with our ideals. We will always lack our ideals. But we will also never be one with our anti-ideals. That, too, is impossible. We lack both ways as human beings. The lacking cancels out and our existence is not one of anguish, but of joy and anguish interpenetrating.

Radical pedagogy refuses to allow alienation to become an ideology. We can become more de-alienated. We can love ourselves and others. We don't hate ourselves, because we don't love ourselves fully. We aren't poor if we are not totally rich

We can approach the ideal of love. The fact of the approachability of the ideal and the recognition of the anti-ideal make our existence *plausible*.

29. Conscience: It all depends what we are conscientious about.

We can be conscientious about the wrong things. So-called sexual improprieties like masturbation represent one example. In trivial education, we are trained to be conscientious only in the most shallow ways. For example, a general regard for our neighbors may be fostered, but the ramifications of this regard are never explained. Part of this general regard will be to treat them according to the precepts of fairness and equality (justice).

As a rule of thumb, conscience should not be wasted on genitalia, but on the oppressive minority that pulls our strings.

Conscience is deflected from serious to trivial concerns or the serious is trivialized by lack of examination of underpinnings. What is conscience for a radical pedagogy?

Because of neutron bombing, icons are expunged in a radical pedagogy of becoming. Only the essential remains: fellow-feeling and thinking. Thinking transcends, posing ever-new doubting-believing. Basic fellow-feeling, or caring, draws me into the lives of others and others into my life. Conscience arises in such primitive fellow-feeling.

30. The Extinction of Teachers and Students:
Every human act involves teaching and learning; thus our
fundamental relationship with others is as both teacher and student.

In typical classrooms, one person (the teacher) knows more (at least in that person's area of expertise) than most of the others (the students). Teachers lead students. Freire calls this "making accessible" to students, but this still amounts to "radial" dialogue. Someone is helping others focus. Verticality with respect to knowledge cannot be eliminated. Verticality with respect to authority can be.

Even assuming teachers do possess more knowledge than students, this does not mean that teachers do not themselves have to be guided in how their knowledge is presented to students. Knowledge remains vivacious to the extent that teachers look to students to guide them to the applicability of the idea. Students have knowledge that teachers lack: the knowledge of how the knowledge is best applicable to them. In encouraging students to teach them, teachers encourage students to question them. In so doing, teachers become students and students teachers.

Yet the primary knowledge comes from teacher-students. Student-teachers furnish complementary knowledge. The knowledge of teacher-students complements the primary knowledge of teacher-students, at least at the beginning of the process within a subject area. Student-teachers move gradually toward becoming teacher-students.

The authority of knowledge should not be confused with professional authority, Freire says. By virtue of being a "teacher" and of having one or more degrees, traditional teachers set up a teacher-student dichotomy that is reminiscent of a master-slave or parent-child dichotomy. In such a dichotomy, someone owns all the knowledge, another is impoverished, without knowledge. The one without knowledge waits for the one with knowledge to deposit it. The relationship between the two is paternalistic. The one with knowledge bestows knowledge to the other, who is supposed to regard it as a gift. The one without knowledge waits passively for the one with knowledge to bestow it. The one with knowledge makes the fundamental decisions, while the one without knowledge waits for those decisions to be made. The one with knowledge is conferred with the status of knowledge-bearer and knowledge-giver; the one without knowledge is conferred with the status of knowledge-taker. Traditional teachers are masters; traditional students slaves, serfs.

Teaching and learning represents the fundamental ontological relationship. We need knowledge from others for our survival. In different relationships, we can be teacher-students or student-teachers. We may be the ones with the knowledge or the ones complementing knowledge. All dialogue with others is one of teaching and learning. At the same time we seek knowledge from others, we also give knowledge to others. Even in the most rudimentary situations, we gain knowledge from others, even if just to ask for directions. The direction-giver, in that instance, is the teacher-student; the recipient of directions, the student-teacher. In the course of questioning the direction-giver may have to adjust the directions to the knowledge of the person wanting directions. If the direction-giver discovers that the person inquiring about directions is a stranger, the directions given will be different from someone who lives in the area. The direction-giver is directed by the person who gives the directions.

What is teaching?

What is learning?

In a radical pedagogy of dynamism, only inquiry remains.

Radical pedagogy recognizes two types of co-inquirers. One initiates initiation in others. Initiation is necessary, which is especially clear where esoteric subjects are concerned. Initiators put their initials on subjects. They do this by naming the subject. The classroom is composed of two types of initiators: teacher-students and student-teachers.

Initiation comes from both sides. Core subject matter comes from initiators, once called "teachers." The Initiator does not patrol the classroom. Initiation into subject matter is met with a concomitant initiation from student-teachers to teacher-students. This amounts to bringing the subject matter to light.

The fundamental intersubjective relationship, which is the basis of all others, is teaching-learning and learning-teaching. If we follow Hegel and Sartre, others are dangerous beings who need to be controlled and enslaved. But any relationship with others is marked by learning-teaching and teaching-learning. We are not merely saying that others are useful to us. If we regard others only in the capacity of learners into which deposits are made, then we do not recognize them as initiators. If we regard them only as depositors, those who convey knowledge, then we reduce them to dispensers of knowledge, treating them as computers, as mere distributors of knowledge. When others are regarded as both initiators and recipients of knowledge, then we treat them as persons. Persons are not pure initiators, nor are they pure recipients. Persons are initiators and recipients. This suggests that persons have needs (for knowledge), but also initiate toward knowledge.

The fundamental ontological relationship in schooling is initiation-initiated. Traditional teachers initiate students into subject matter. Traditional students are "being initiated." The initiation comes from one side. In a radical pedagogy of dynamism, initiation and being initiated comes from both sides. Teacher-students initiate student-teachers into subject matter and classroom "philosophy." Student-teachers initiate teacher-students into their relative level of knowledge as well their interests with respect to the subject matter.

When teaching-learning verticality is removed, so is the dominator-dominated verticality. Knowledge is no longer foisted on others. Teachers can no longer overpower students with knowledge, any more than the rich should overpower the poor. The traditional teacher-student relationship reminds me of the rich-poor relationship in capitalistic society. The rich allow only crumbs to trickle down to the poor, so that the poor can only survive and not flourish. Whatever the poor receive, it is for the express purpose of subjugation. Only a few miracles make it out of poverty. Miracles are considered hard workers and are pets of the rich. The rich never intend to allow the poor to become rich. The point is to keep them poor.

In general, the poor shall always remain poor. And students shall always remain students. The point is to keep students in their ignorant state. Traditional teachers keep students in ignorance, no matter how many facts they give them. They keep students in ignorance by feeding them facts. Fact distribution does not free students, any more than welfare frees the poor. It makes the poor dependent on the rich. Traditional teachers cannot hope to cultivate initiation in their students unless the traditional classroom is supplanted by the problem-posing classroom. Initiators cannot arise in the traditional classroom. To ask for initiation from students without first restructuring authority is a blueprint for failure.

To desire initiation, whether from students or the poor, demands the relinquishing of dominance and authority. It presupposes equality. Such equality means that everybody is initiator and recipient (being initiated). Everyone is both teacher and student.

31. Peace: Initiation culminates in peace.

Dialogue may include antagonism. It may include hurt feelings, fear, or dismay. This is because dialogue inherently consists of questioning, which mirrors the transcendence of thinking. The questioning comes from all sides. Initiators negotiate and thus cooperate in identifying and creating the object of knowledge. All are treated as spontaneous and receptive beings. We call this common inquiry Peace.

32. Holism: Compartmentalized thinking stifles dynamism.

Belief in holism suggests belief that people can make interconnections. Belief in compartmentalization suggests the contrary belief: people cannot make interconnections. This is a fundamental pedagogical point: Do we believe that most persons can see beyond facts or between them?

Compartmentalized schooling goes hand-in-hand with the banking concept of education. Knowledge offered piecemeal without cultivating initiation leaves the students without a clue with respect to making connections. Compartmentalized schooling keeps students in the dark. Darkness fades to the extent that we go beyond facts and invent and create interconnections.

On its most simple level, holism pushes us beyond facts and compels us to compare facts. Holism cultivates more than ingestion of facts. It cultivates thinking because it is thinking. Thinking is an act of transcendence. Holistic thinking, then, is natural. Compartmentalized thinking is unnatural. It attempts to make discrete unchangeable facts rather than demonstrating the dynamism of thinking.

Compartmentalized knowledge works in conjunction with the banking concept of education to mystify the process of schooling. From this perspective, teachers distribute discrete facts to students. Teachers control the distribution of facts, carefully deciding what will and what won't be within the parameters of "appropriate" discussion. A dichotomy is set up between the knower and the ignorant. The knower must always be known as the knower, not as anything else. The knower's authority is based on possessing all the knowledge, just as the ignorant person's lack of authority is based on lacking any knowledge. In no way can the knower's monopoly on knowledge be jeopardized. This means that genuine questioning must be absent. For genuine questioning would undermine the authority of the teacher as absolute knower.

Integrative thinking introduces challenges to the absolute knower because it forces inquiry out of the bounds of a subject or area of specialization. Pushing the inquiry out of bounds jeopardizes the absolute knower. The absolute knower becomes a knower among knowers, involved in negotiation. Dialoguing de-emphasizes the one-way transferal of knowledge and creates opportunities for everybody to become spontaneous and receptive learners.

33. Differences and Indifference:
Having differences is not the same as being different.

Egocentrism states that a person views the world only from her or his perspective.[6] Ethnocentrism states that a group only views the world from the group's perspective. Egocentrism and ethnocentrism are a looking at the world from a single frame of reference. This does not entail that different people outside this frame of reference cannot look at the world from this frame of reference. The presumption is that others can and should understand. This is not the case with respect to separacentrism. Separacentrism states that a group only sees the world from a single point and that "different" groups can never fathom this frame of reference. Experiences of the group are invisible to and untranslatable to other groups. Untranslatability of experience is characteristic of separacentrism, whereas it is not characteristic of egocentrism or ethnocentrism.

Separacentrism hinders dialogue from occurring between oppressed groups. Separacentrism is a divide-and-rule strategy that transforms "having differences" into "being different." "Having differences" connotes the continuation of dialogue, even in the friction of difference. "Being different" assumes that different groups have essential differences that prevent communication and cooperation. "Being different" is the essence of separacentrism. Focusing on "being different," separacentrism is indifferent to other oppressed groups. No communication, no dialogue, no understanding, no cooperation with other oppressed groups. The focus is on "being different" instead of "having differences." If the focus is on "being different" rather than "having differences," then divide-and-rule has been successful.

In a radical pedagogy of dynamism, our goal should be to prevent dialogue on "having differences" from becoming a monologue on "being different." This does not endorse the naive sentiment of the oppressor: "We are all human or we are all Americans; you oppressed can be just like us." Such an invitation to join "us" is less an invitation for the oppressed group to join, and more grabbing a few individuals of the group who can be co-opted and used to maintain the status quo. This is nothing more than a false invitation of inclusion, another enticement, like the Horatio Alger myth. Such invitations from the dominant group to oppressed groups are at best tepid. When the oppressor says to the oppressed "You are human like us, you are not different" this is less affirmation of the humanity of the oppressed, and more a denial of culpability in the of the oppressed.

The United States is steering toward a pluralism of "being different" rather than a pluralism of "having differences." If this continues, then alliances between oppressed groups will be less likely and the status quo will remain unchallenged. Accordingly, a pedagogy of radical dynamism de-emphasizes "being different" and emphasizes "having differences." The first is anti-dialogical, the second dialogical.

Let us examine the lexical definitions of "to differ," "difference," and "different." According to the *Oxford English Dictionary*, the verb "differ" means "to make unlike, dissimilar, or distinct; to have contrary or diverse bearings, tendencies, or qualities; to be unlike, diverse, or various in nature, form, or qualities, or in some specified respect, to have differences; to quarrel." The noun "difference" means the condition, quality, or fact of being different or not the same in quality or in essence. The adjective "different" means having characters or qualities that diverge from one another, of another, nature, form, or quality, in a weaker sense, used as a synonym for *other,* as denying identity, but without any implication of dissimilarity. "Difference" can mean not having the same quality in essence or it can mean the denial of identity without implying dissimilarity. Difference can connote having a different essence or nature from the other (being different); or it can connote non-identity without implying dissimilarity (having differences). I suggest that "being different" lays the groundwork for indifference.

In the *Phenomenology of Spirit*, Hegel explains the experience of the alien or unfamiliar.[7] When we first confront the unfamiliar, the alien, we resist it to preserve our insights. The unfamiliar challenges our autonomy and is therefore disquieting.

In the famous section on "Master-Slave" section of the *Phenomenology*, Hegel describes how two consciousness come into conflict with one another.[8] One must conquer the other in order to gain the other's acknowledgment. The single consciousness is fearful after recognizing that the egocentric world around it is false and intrinsically based on intersubjectivity. Consciousness engages in a duel of death with the Other to maintain its identity. In this conflict, one consciousness becomes the master, the other the slave. Our pedagogy of dynamism rejects meeting with others as a struggle for dominance. Because we view ourselves as "differing," in the very nature of our thinking, we can more readily accept difference.

Difference need not be seen as coming into conflict with others. In *Lesbian Ethics,* Sarah Hoagland offers an alternative to the Hegelian model. In the experience of difference, people can see to what degrees each is being oppressed.[9] In contrast to merging, the experience of difference points out boundaries between people, helping them to see that their agendas are not identical. Fear of difference prevents us from attending to one another. We can only connect with difference when we give up control, when we allow ourselves to be enhanced by the unfamiliar instead of being destroyed by it. Openness to being enhanced by difference stands in stark contrast to the Hegelian model. Being open to change requires a measure of confidence that we will not be corrupted by difference. We have this measure of confidence because we consider ourselves as creative beings who can reshape our perspectives if they are challenged.

The accounts of difference by Hegel and Hoagland can be incorporated into an analysis of difference from the perspectives of both the oppressor and the oppressed.

Oppressors and oppressed see difference much differently. Difference does not endanger them. Difference can be enjoyed because it is not a threat. Difference can be viewed at a distance. Difference can be avoided. Difference can be co-opted, controlled. Difference can be chosen. Difference does not force itself on the oppressors. Difference does not invade oppressors. Oppressors can see difference as enhancing their being.

The oppressed see difference as a threat to their being. They have been made, far of all, to feel different. As Freire says in *Pedagogy of the Oppressed,* cultural invasion denigrates the oppressed putting tags like "inferior," "ingrates," "shiftess," "diseased," and "mixed blood" on them.[10] Oppressors dehumanize the oppressed with these differences, emphasizing the oppressed "being different." These differences serve to alienate the oppressed. This difference is put upon the oppressed by their oppressors. The oppressed keenly feel their difference. Difference to them is an opprobrium, a badge of dishonor and disgrace. This is not a difference that they have chosen. This is a difference of degradation. Difference is experienced as alienating, not enhancing. The oppressed undergo great psychological pain and struggle to free themselves of this fear or conflict with difference. This is why they are double-souled or ambiguous beings. However, if that time of development is manipulated and disfigured, as is the case in the oppressor-oppressed relationship, then "having differences" becomes "being different." Oppressors can confidently dwell within difference because they possess the power and ability to control and create difference.

The oppressed are made to feel difference in every aspect of their lives: economically, aesthetically, politically, and socially. Having internalized these differences, some of the oppressed want to belong to the oppressor class. Many amply wallow in self-hating self-image. Their being different is a negative thing.

Difference is unavoidable. Difference cannot be chosen. Difference is not distant; difference is embedded in the oppressed. As the oppressor exorcises the image of the oppressed, a new kind of difference emerges. This is a difference that wants no intellectual intercourse with other differences. It is so sick of being invaded by differences that it longer wants difference. It is unrelated difference; it is indifference.

The exhaustion and trauma arising from the destruction of the oppressor's poison leave the weakened body to focus only on itself and its recuperation. It then affirms its own "being different" making itself unique and the center of the universe. In the process, it may turn the tables and depreciate its oppressors, via an inversion of values. Or it may opt for unrelatedness (or so it believes). Hegel's "law of the heart" is applicable here. Persons following the "law of the heart" find their hearts divided and only are able to maintain their own standards by depreciating the public standards that they (like others) covertly acknowledge.[11] This conflict in values leads to self-hatred and also hatred of others.

What is the rationale for separatism? Let us examine separatism from a lesbian perspective. Many Lesbians do not want their feelings and judgments challenged; they need space for their feelings. Being challenged by the oppressor will stifle self-development. We see this rationale used with respect to all-female or all-black schools. According to Hoagland, separation is necessary to avoid demoralization. Without separation, Lesbians (1) cannot be moral agents outside the dominant/subordinate framework of heterosexuality; (2) lose the focus of their anger and desire to de-politicize these emotions, which are redirected into scapegoating; (3) deny their oppressed status; and (4) lose belief they can make a difference.[12] Hoagland sees separatism as positive only if it is not simply a separatism for survival, but is a separation for diversity and growth. Hoagland, like Freire, recognizes that reform is another form of co-optation. She criticizes feminist reforms because their focus is on men: such reforms address men's conceptions of women, not women's values. She also contends that feminist reforms depend on men to bring about change. Finally, the focus is on the value change in men rather than the value change in women. Hoagland's fundamental point throughout is that lesbian self-definition cannot be accomplished in the heterosexual community and that co-optation is equally pernicious to that aim. Lesbians must withdraw from the existing ground of meaning to refocus on a lesbian framework. Community must not arise because of outside threats or traditions, but according the belief that we can enact our own values. Separatism is a refusal to act according to the oppressor's system. In withdrawing from the system, separatists refuse to energize it. This withdrawal is a form of engagement that can topple the system. In the final analysis, as W.E.B. DuBois points out, separation may be necessary for the survival of a group, to prevent spiritual and physical disaster.[13] But as Martin Luther King, Jr. contends, minorities like Blacks gain strength only by forming coalitions with other groups.[14]

Can separatism contribute to the demise of the oppressors? Is Hoagland right when she says that when the couriers refuse to deliver the messages of the king, then the king is left powerless?[15] This analogy needs to be restructured in order to be congruent with reality in a pluralistic society. We see that many different couriers exist in a pluralistic society (besides the postal service, United Parcel Service, Federal Express, and other similar couriers, the phone companies, Internet, etc.). If one of the couriers resists, then what does it matter to the king? The king can always use the other couriers. If some of the couriers resist, but not cohesively, then that too, won't bring about the demise of the king. Only by forming a coalition of couriers (who resist by withdrawing their services) will the king's power be challenged. Where did the Million Man March lead? Where did the March on Washington lead (even though Malcolm called it "The Farce on Washington")? Separatism may lead to short-term self-affirmation, but by its very definition is insignificant in the revolution against the forces that are oppressing the affirmation.

Separatism is often necessary for the survival of a group. The group must put up walls to defend themselves from destructive alien influence. The dominant powers want separatism, for this insures divisiveness. The ultimate goal of oppressors is separation among the oppressed. At the extreme, oppressed groups whose very survival depends upon separation are justified in separating. This separation is justified in the same way an abused spouse justified from separating from an abusive partner. If self-survival depends upon separation, separation is justified. It does play into the hands of the divide-and-conquer strategy of the oppressors. We might want to refer to this as the "Babel strategy." When God wanted to prevent the building of the Tower of Babel, the Lord made all the workers speak in different languages. Unable to communicate with one another, all work stopped and the workers quarreled among themselves. Cooperative ventures become difficult in a climate of separatism. In some sense, we have to know how to speak different languages and not simply our own. We can have cooperation among those groups who are justified in their separation. To speak in a "different voice," to borrow from the title of Carol Gilligan's famous book, but not so different that we cannot hear each other. If each separate group speaks in different voices that are untranslatable to Others, then dialogue is impossible.

When people have differences, they differ in opinion. "Having differences" does not mean the same as "being different." "Having differences" suggests that the dialogue continues even though parties disagree. I can have differences with you, but that does not mean that we cannot dialogue. "Having differences" still connotes a process, although perhaps an antagonistic one. "Having differences" is an act directed toward others, including others. "Being different" does not connote process. "Being different" connotes essential differences. Such differences can never be reconciled. "Being different" takes the oppressed group into isolation and without any relatedness to other oppressed groups. "Having differences" suggests antagonism but also relatedness. "Being different" means an essence not related to other essences. This represents indifference. "Having differences" is the basis for continued dialogue; "being different" is the basis for no such interaction. "Being different" is separation from a shared humanity. "Being different" is an alienation from other human beings of different groups. "Being different" prevents groups from "having differences." "Being different" is the essence of indifference.

We can describe indifference as Hegel does, as a "simple togetherness of plurality" in which properties are "indifferent to another, each is on its own and free from the others," each being "a simple relating of self to self" leaving "the others alone . . . connected with them only by the indifferent Also."[16] The universal holding together of these properties is thinghood. Looking at the properties of salt in this way, we see its properties (White, tart cubical) are in the same place (the simple Here), but "they do not affect each other in this interpenetration."[17] "The whiteness does not affect the cubical shape, and neither affects the tart taste, etc."[18] Hegel explains.

If we relate this idea to separacentrism, we have the following scenario. Blacks, Jews, Lesbians, etc., relating only themselves to themselves, held together by an abstraction (thinghood). While existing in the same Here (the United States), they are indifferent to one another. In this vision of the United States, different groups are bound together by an indifferent Also. Hegel says that "the Thing is the *Also,* or the *universal medium* in which the many properties subsist from another, without touching or canceling one another."[19] This represents an isolationism within the same country, an internal isolationism. If white, tart, and cubical are indifferent to one another in the salt, so Blacks, Jews, Lesbians are indifferent to one another in the United States.

This is sham indifference. Hegel demonstrates that the qualities of the salt must exist in relation to one another in order to exist at all. So, too, Blacks, Jews, and Lesbians must exist in relation to one another. The essence of salt, what it means to be salt, consists of its color, shape, and taste. Salt is less than salt without any of its essential features. The same applies to human relationships and human communities. The make-up of the society of the United States consists of many different groups. In a similar fashion, the make-up of the individual groups is also dependent upon outside groups for its creation. What it means to be Black is in part what it means for Blacks to associate with Whites. The same can be said for Lesbians or any other group within the United States. This is why separatism, which leads to separacentrism, fails. We cannot avoid relationships. Indifferent pluralism promotes an ideology of "being different." Interactive pluralism promotes an ideology of "having differences." The ideology of "being different" is: "We only care about how we look at the world; the way you look at it is your business, but we don't really care that much how you look at it." Separacentrism lays the groundwork for absolutism that can only be known by or revealed to the separated group.

Another problem inherent with separacentrism is intellectual incest and knowledge xenophobia. The more pronounced the separation, the less intercourse with "different" points-of-view, then the more knowledge xenophobia. This can be exemplified by the plight of Jews of the sixteenth, seventeenth, and eighteenth centuries. Separacentrism is the basis for intellectual incest and xenophobia Had Martin Luther King, Jr. been separacentric, then would he have found the works of Gandhi, or even cared whether such a person existed and what strategies this person proposed to challenge an oppressive regime? Had Paulo Freire been separacentric, would *Pedagogy of the Oppressed* be a medley of "different" perspectives?

In the same way capitalism blurs the distinction between needs and whims and collapses the latter into the former, so the pedagogy of the oppressors blurs the distinction between "being different" and "having differences" and collapses the one into the other. Let us look at the tendencies in this country, one of which is "different" groups flying away from each other at seemingly great speeds. It might as well be that these different groups dwell in different counties or on different planets for that matter. Each group wants nothing to do with other groups. They have no desire to discern difference.

In such a case, the dominant group has successfully divided and conquered. The dominant group stays in power, while different oppressed groups fight among themselves and emphasize their differences. The affirmation of "being different" plays right into the "divide-and-conquer" strategy. It lays the groundwork of true indifference, of profound alienation. Under such circumstances, without hope, without trust, without commonality, deep change is not possible.

The function of intellectuals of oppressed groups is complex. One their chief functions is to create ways to expel the graven images of the oppressor from the souls of their people. This is essential for self-determination. Yet this is not the only duty. Intellectuals must be more far-sighted than believing that expulsion of the oppressors' image is their sole goal. To prevent *intellectual* inertia and intellectual incest from becoming rampant intellectuals of oppressed groups must seek other ways of knowing. This can greatly benefit the oppressed.

Intellectuals who are strictly "centric" do a disservice to their group. "Being different" is not a basis for dialogue. As Freire says, dialogue is the movement toward the continued humanization of others. It would be a wonderful trick to humanize others by ignoring them. The continued personalization or humanization of others depends on the premise that others are human or persons. The rhetoric of "being different" stifles dialogue, creating more and more distance between oppressed groups such that they cannot hear one another and view themselves as unrelated to one another.

The pervasive nihilism of our era is not the result of the "death of God," as existentialists are fond of saying, We can endure the death of God. What we cannot endure is the death of dialogue. Dialogue is based on love, hope, trust, and faith in other people. The death of dialogue means the "death of other people": Our lack of love for them, our lack of faith and trust in them, hopelessness with respect to creating common ground, alienates one from the other to such a great extent that we cannot communicate. And without communication, others dissolve into (to twist a verbalism of our day) virtual unreality.

34. Spontaneity: When you kill spontaneity, you kill thinking.

When we think about images of thinking, we think about Socrates or some other classical thinker. There is Socrates, chin in the palm of his hand, meditating, ruminating, masticating. This gives us the impression that thinking is slow and plodding. Thinking takes a long time, and we must never jump to conclusions. Thinking is like fine wine: it cannot be rushed.

What has just been described cannot be counted as, in any way, shape, or form, as spontaneity. Spontaneity is the contrary to mastication. Spontaneity suggests a certain rapidity. Spontaneity suggests "jumping" to conclusions and in a sense a kind of "rushing."

Spontaneity never has a chance to occur according to the Socratic image for thinking. Everything is reduced to slow motion. Everything must be chewed a thousand times before it is ready to be considered a thought. Only the most deeply hewn reflection is worthy of being called a "thought."

This does not speak to the origin of thinking. Thinking begins in bits and spurts. If allowed to proceed in a spontaneous fashion, thinking can fly into many different directions. Dialogue fosters the spontaneity of thinking. Half-baked ideas emerge in the dialogue. Yes, the ideas may be half-baked. Some of them at some future date may become full-baked. Let us always remember that full-baked ideas were once half-baked. Spontaneity allows for the inclusion of our most basic intuitions concerning the world. Spontaneity is the fluidity of thinking. Spontaneity, because it is less "reflective," allows us to make connections we might not normally make. This is because in this less reflective state, we are less bound by conventions.

Without spontaneity, thinking never occurs. Thinking involves throwing ourselves into contradictions and then attempting to find our way out of them.

Spontaneity and flashes of insight (intuition) fit together. Mastication inertizes the thinking process. The fits and starts of thinking are removed. The fits and starts of thinking are primarily the flashes of insight. Mastication is the water thrown on flashes of insight.

This is not to say that mastication has no place in the process of thinking. Mastication is primarily for the elaboration of or systematization of insights. Systematization simply for the sake of systematization is banal.

The banal is the anal. Thinking does not begin by trying to build a system. Systems creep out of insights. The web of systematization is spun from one or more insights.

The image of the wise person on top of the mountaintop, meditating, is not the idea that I believe appropriate for thinking. Great thoughts occur only after many bad thoughts are born. The old model aborts thoughts before they are born. The new model has a large litter of thoughts and allows them to subjected to continual questioning.

The image I believe best captures thinking is the person in dialogue with others. Dialogue is filled with stops and starts, with glitches, with half-baked ideas, with an occasional glimmer of insight that can be the basis for further reflection.

Thinking does not begin in light. Thinking begins in ambiguity. Thinking begins as soon as the contradictions, paradoxes, and ambiguities of our views become apparent. In such messiness, thinking arises. Things have become messy because of the spontaneity of our thinking.

Without leaving room for spontaneity, we thereby leave little or no room for insight. If everything is planned, as within a system, then we leave no room for the unplanned.

That is what insights are: they are unplanned. They come upon us. They are revelations.

We spontaneously move from thought to thought. This is sometimes called the stream of consciousness (although stream of self-consciousness would be more accurate). Reflective systematization, to reiterate, is also necessary for thinking. Here, we are careful to detect contradictions in our thinking and formalizing interconnections.

Flashes of insight may be nothing more than mirages. They may be nothing. But these flashes are the foundation on which genuine thinking is made.

The classroom founded on spontaneity is extremely dangerous to the traditional teacher. If anything can be thought, then anything can be said. Should teacher-students think spontaneously, then perhaps unformed thoughts will be presented to student-teachers, who will then find reason to criticize and compel teacher-students to develop them.

35. Error: Faith in error is faith in the spontaneity of thinking.

A pedagogy of dynamism must not simply allow for error, in the way that we tolerate annoying little things. Error is not a pest, either to be eliminated or shooed away. Error is essential to truthbearing.

Most schooling regards errors as pests. Teachers are like those electric insect lights in the backyard. They draw insects toward them and then fry them. This is what traditional teachers do. By virtue of their authority, they draw students in close only to fry them for their errors.

A pedagogy of dynamism must embrace error as much as it embraces truth. Making room for spontaneity of thinking demands that mistakes not be punished, as if they were capital crimes. The more mistakes, the clearer things become because we see better what something is not. By seeing what something is not, we begin to see what it is.

Cultivating spontaneity is the most important thing in cultivating thinking. The development of spontaneity cannot occur when people are constantly told to stop and to address their errors. This is not to say that errors should not be addressed. How and when the errors are addressed remains the key issue. It is an error and a cardinal sin to disrupt the flow of thinking. Belief in the native intelligence of human beings means faith that people will be able to spot their own errors.

This goes against the grain of most schooling. Learning the facts kills learning, my pedagogic creed states. Cultivating the flow of learning cultivates self-learning, self-initiation.

This does not mean that no facts should be taught students. This does not mean that we stop at error and applaud it. Instead, allow students to make a hundred errors on their own than be correct on the basis of following what the teacher said.

The whole point of schooling is the cultivation of initiation. Initiation is stifled when the making mistakes or committing errors is deemed crimes. Spontaneity is killed. You end up with a bunch of students who are afraid to make their thoughts known for fear of making an error.

You are advocating people running around in a fog. My, you are perverse. Advocating error. That is anarchy, pure and simple.

A pedagogic creed of dynamism begins in the fog because it believes people can dwell in fogginess. The other perspective places people in sunlight because it believes that people are too dull to find their way out of the fog.

A pedagogic creed of dynamism begins in the fog for another reason as well. The fog is what thinking is. In the fog, in the ambiguous fog, thinking occurs. Thinking never takes place in the sunshine. Only as we weave our way through the fog, and negotiate toward what we believe to be truth, do we become critical thinkers.

Only as we act on the world do we understand it. Our thinking is necessarily connected with our action. In our actions, we make mistakes. We mistake this for something else. Without the process of making error, truth in any real sense cannot be ascertained. The ascertained truth will shallow and insignificant without affirming error. In a radical pedagogy, action is embraced, even if it results in errors.

Negotiations are fraught with error. Common ground is hard to establish. One side may be too extreme, another not extreme enough. We negotiate toward truth. We try to find a view in which many key contradictions can be solved. But in solving a set of contradictions, we create others.

36. Open-Mindedness: God is the only being who is close-minded.

Human beings are naturally open-minded. They are naturally doubting Teresas and Thomases. The inherent nature of self-consciousness assures this open-mindedness. Every belief is tinged by doubt. This doubting is the basis for open-mindedness.

God never doubts. God possesses absolute knowledge. God is close-minded because of the completeness of God's knowledge. Human beings always doubt. Every truth is thrown into doubt. This is because of our fundamental incompleteness of knowledge. Human beings attempt to view things with a false certainty. We attempt to deny.

What is the chief means of removing doubt?

The primary way is to discourage open-mindedness or doubt concerning our position is to employ the banking concept of education. For bankers, doubt is minimized because of an absence of dialogue. Dialogue stirs up doubt, allowing as it does the introduction of many viewpoints. In the banking concept of education, only one viewpoint matters. Students must conform to this omnipotent perspective.

In dialogue, we are constantly reminded of the incompleteness of our knowledge. This in turn lays the groundwork for doubt. As long as we doubt, we can say that we are open-minded. And we cannot help doubting.

Many people cannot live in ambiguity. They want to erase ambiguity. They attempt to sterilize thinking. They want everything to fit into little niches. Open-mindedness cannot exist in an atmosphere of certainty.

The open-minded view everything as a question. This means that something could be possibly this or possibly that.

Open-mindedness is philosophy. Even first principles can be challenged. All religions, all religions without exception, are bastions of close-mindedness. We use the term "narrow-mindedness" because we do not think close-mindedness is possible except for God. Narrow-mindedness, undoubtedly, but not close-mindedness. All human beings are prone to doubt.

37. Common Sense: Never wish common sense on anybody.

Common sense is supposed to be a good thing. Common sense tells us: Don't throw the baby out with the bath water.

I disagree with and disavow such a mistaken notion.

Many persons contrast common sense with esoteric knowledge. Common sense applies to the practical affairs and is down to earth. Abstract knowledge is inapplicable to practical affairs and is in the clouds somewhere. Common sense pertains to the common person. Abstract or theoretical knowledge is accessible only to a learned few. But abstract knowledge has only marginal value, and no value to the common person. While the common person lacks esoteric knowledge, the learned person lacks common sense.

What is most important?

Common sense.

The esoteric stuff applies only to a limited and relatively unimportant sphere. Common sense applies to the widest and most important spheres of our lives. Common sense is equated with the way of the world, of being able to succeed in the world.

What is wrong with this conception of common sense?

Common sense is deemed more valuable than esoteric knowledge. In fact, common sense is the most desired sort of knowledge. Theoretical knowledge is despised for its apparent inapplicability. Common-sense arguments are based on the argument's apparent utility or absence of utility. If the utility of an argument can be seen, then it is only common sense. If the utility of the argument cannot immediately be seen, the argument lacks merit.

Common sense often sets itself against metaphysical knowledge. Common sense knowledge is rooted in experience. It is hostile to anything beyond experience, as, for example, the fundamental model of self-consciousness that I have employed. Common sense is opposed to the possible.

Common sense is not basing our judgments on sense perception. It also refers to accepting the "self-evident" truths or ideology of a culture. Whatever the predominant beliefs of a society, they become part of the body of common sense. In other words, "everybody should believe it, it's so obvious even a child could see."

Whatever becomes part of the dogma of common sense becomes the unchallenged. It becomes what I term "religion." Common-sense beliefs are self-evident, unassailable first principles. Whatever contradicts common sense must be false. If it is "common sense" that anybody can possess the American Dream, then anybody who says otherwise is wrong, especially those who address the issue with non-common sense arguments.

Common-sense arguments never descend into ambiguity. They cannot; for ambiguity would render them open to question. Common sense can be an ideological tactic meant to limit the parameters of discussion. Common sense will not allow contradictions to abound. This would ruin the "obvious" simple truth of common-sense beliefs.

Appeals to common sense are not appeals to dialogue. Such a statement may appear to be extremely harsh, but actually is not. Common sense draws limits to discussion. Discussion must be conducted within the parameters of common sense. I refuse to use the word "dialogue" in conjunction with common sense. Dialogue entertains all possibilities. Common sense narrows dialogue.

Common sense squares with empiricism. Empiricists are often the biggest advocates of common sense. By this, they mean appealing to experience. A pedagogy of dynamism also appeals to experience. But what it means by experience and what empiricists mean by experience are different. Empiricists point to sense experience as the validation of their claims. My radical pedagogy begins from the standpoint of human self-consciousness. It looks at the meaning of our experience, in the tradition of phenomenology. I established that a pedagogy of becoming can be based on self-consciousness. This allowed me to elaborate a pedagogy not based on sense perceptions or neurons, but on the interpenetration of subject and object. This allowed me to uncover the basic structure of thinking, which I believe is crucial to a pedagogy of radical pedagogy.

Common sense often leads back to the dominant ideology of a society. People may point to the American revolutionaries who advocated "common sense." Their "common sense" involved a critical analysis of the dominant ideology; thus, it was not common sense.

Hume's easy and obvious philosophy resembles a common-sense vision of the world. But Hume takes one of the most radical positions in the history of philosophy: that cause and effect have no necessary connection and are loose and separate. This is hardly the conventional or common sense way of looking at the world. This shocking perspective is hardly "easy and obvious."

Hume does not discover anything about the nature of things. He discovers something about self-consciousness. He discovers that nothing is certain and that everything is possible. When he says that the contrary of every matter of fact is always possible, he makes a statement not about the world, but about self-consciousness.

Radical pedagogy does not always reject views that are held in common. It all depends on the process by which those views are held in common. Most of the time, views held in common are the result of inherited beliefs. We believe in something because it is part of tradition. Common sense is often congealed knowledge, or a traditional mode of viewing the world.

Dialogue is central to a pedagogy of dynamism. If we develop a common view from dialogue, this is not the same as the common sense views we inherit. For in dialogue, we negotiate toward truth. Negotiation is a process toward the truth. Through a negotiation of diverse perspectives, we reach toward truth.

Appeals to common sense are not the same as negotiating toward truth. Appeals to experience are not enough to bring forth the truth. The truth is brought forth in negotiation with other viewpoints. The truth does not appear through common sense. Common sense is anchored by the historical weight of traditions and prevalent ideological assumptions. Common sense merely conceals value-laden assumptions from view, for example, not throwing the baby out with the bath water.

38. Suspension of Judgment: We can suspend students, not judgments.

A pedagogy of dynamism refuses to accept the popular notion of suspension of judgment. Our minds can no less judge than our eyes can see.

Judgments are made on the most basic level. When something is presented to us, whether it be a statement by somebody or an event, we either believe or disbelieve it. You tell me something and either I believe it or don't believe it. I believe that those kids holding hands in class are in love, but don't believe the lightning and thunder are portents of the end of the world. We can say we won't judge. But that is like saying: Our eyes are open and we are looking, but we are not judging. Suspension of judgment is not possible.

We are judges.

The transcending nature of self-consciousness renders suspension of judgment We cannot throw off this believing-non-believing posture. Doubting is not the same thing as suspending our judgment. Doubting does not imply a nonjudgmental attitude. When we say, "We doubt Jonah's story that he had sex fourteen times last night between the hours of midnight and three," we disbelieve Jonah's story. Doubting represents a judgment against a belief.

On the level of value, we also judge. We are immediately drawn to or repulsed by the values we find in things. Put in the most basic terms: we love or hate whatever appears to us. Even when we find nothing particularly attractive or repulsive in something, we say that it is "blah," "boring," or "mediocre."

These are value judgments. When push comes to shove, we cannot stifle this primitive valuing any more than we can not see this sentence. Rather than suspending judgments, which we have demonstrated is not possible, we should assess our judgments in another way.

The myth of suspending judgments is pernicious. Under the guise of suspension of belief, we may assume that we can set aside our biases and look at the world "objectively." Such objectivity is supposed to be "value-free." Rather than deny value-judgments, we must recognize the types of value judgment we make. We must seek the ideological assumptions that guide our thinking. Many of the ideological assumptions are common-sense statements such as "survival of the fittest," "competition as good," or "I only care about something if it happens to me."

Instead of feigning suspension of belief, pedagogy should be aimed at the disclosure of belief. A comprehensive understanding of ourselves is vital. Yet self-understanding merges with an understanding of our society. We know ourselves only to the extent we know others and our society and other societies as well. Understanding is holistic.

How is the understanding cultivated? Today, we say by cultivating critical thinking skills. But the rudiments of our thinking are within thinking itself. Dewey says that human beings naturally infer. We naturally want to know things. We make inferences because gaps that emerge in our thinking need to be woven together. This weaving together or synthesizing is understanding.

When we understand anything, we see the understood thing at a distance. This distancing is accomplished by following the natural flow of self-consciousness. A pedagogy of dynamism is not didactic, but pushes us back to examine the flow of thinking.

Suspension of judgment often occurs at the exclusion of our feelings. Such repression or marginalization of feelings conceals knowledge. For knowledge is not simply abstract reasoning, but always reason merging with emotions.

39. Freedom and Dynamism: Freedom is philosophy.

Frequently, our biggest oppressors are ourselves, although we could not have done such a good job without the help of others. We live in an oppressive world in which we unknowingly internalize the images of our oppressors and become oppressors ourselves. Finding the oppressor within requires dialogue. Dialogue discloses a vast web of interconnections and our place within this network. We must know our place in the world to grasp the nature of our oppression.

Our freedom consists in identifying our oppressors and then acting to eliminate the source of oppression. Exorcising demons is crucial to a pedagogy of dynamism. Knowing thyself comes down to knowing thy oppressors. The way we face and value the world is largely within the framework of oppression.

Awareness of self requires political and social awareness. We know ourselves to the extent we know our society and other societies. I am not suggesting that self-awareness is some sort of group consciousness. Nietzsche and Kierkegaard believe that truth cannot not emerge in the market place, among the rabble, the television watchers who are in love with their remote controls. The herd is apish. The point is not to follow blindly the herd and their mad dash to petty pleasures. But we can never forget the impact of the market place.

Freedom consists of freedom from icons and a capacity to create new world visions. Freedom is philosophy, for philosophy is the breaker of icons.

Freedom cannot be conceived only as an act of an individual. A person is free only to the extent that all others are free, so the slogan goes. The freedom of all implies a world without oppression. In such a world, people would be able to make their own decisions and determine their own lives.

Hence, a pedagogy of dynamism cultivates freedom not on an individual basis, but on both individual and collective levels.

40. Affirmation of Dynamism: We affirm dynamism by affirming thinking.

We best cultivate a pedagogy of dynamism by focusing our attention on thinking. If we allow thinking to go on its natural path, people will become more "comfortable" with the discomfort involved in thinking. Dynamism can be affirmed to the extent that thinking can be affirmed. When we freeze concepts and deny the fluidity of thinking (of course, this denial is fruitless because of the doubt-belief continuum inherent in self-consciousness), we tend not to accept the insecurity that accompanies the experience of the different.

Being afraid of the dynamism is at base a fear of becoming different than what we are at this moment. Those who desire inert ideas cherish sameness. They fear that inert ideas will suddenly become dynamic and become other than what they are (different).

Affirmation of difference of others stems from affirmation of ourselves as difference. A pedagogy of radical dynamism must cultivate an understanding of self-consciousness in order to cultivate acceptance of difference in ourselves and in others. We must be able to accept ourselves as different from ourselves in the process of thinking and living. We must accept that we are alien to ourselves inasmuch as we never know what we are going to think or what we are going to be. We understand the alien in others to the extent that we understand the alien in ourselves.

How do we create common ground in all this difference? Our thinking uncovers essential differences: up and down, justice and injustice, being and not-being, equality and inequality, pleasure and displeasure. An essence is never solitary, but always has a mate, a difference. Believing-doubting is the essence of thinking.

Thinking is always uprootedness. This uprootedness always brings us back to rootedness.

A pedagogy of dynamism promotes positive peace. Positive peace is requisite for the full development of thinking. Positive peace pertains to a social situation that is orderly and just. In the banking concept of education, order is unjust. Orderly transferals of knowledge that do not endanger the hierarchy of teacher-student, employer-employee, ruler-leader are the rule. Order is no measure of justice. An unjust order can be efficient and orderly. Oppression is employed to preserve the order. Privilege is accorded to the ruling class, while an absence of rights is characteristic of the oppressed.

Negative peace requires an order and command system that eliminates all ambiguity. Order and command clearly convey the necessary "truths" that the stupid people need in order to serve the dominating class. Ambiguity is a great enemy of negative peace. Ambiguity provides opportunities for thinking.

Those who advocate negative peace are anxious about the destructive rebellion that could occur were the rabble to think and have "too much freedom." The notion of "too much freedom" frightens those who have little or no faith in their creativity or the creativity of others.

In a pedagogy of radical dynamism, ambiguity is necessary for promoting thinking. Ambiguity naturally occurs; it does not have to be artificially inseminated into the classroom. Only within the negative peace of the banking classroom is ambiguity denied. Only within the positive peace of the radical classroom is peace egalitarian and democratic. This peace is sustained in dialogue.

Negative peace dovetails with the myth of clarity and faithlessness in the creativity of others. In negative peace, the majority of people are deprived of "truths" and their thinking is stifled by manipulative bankers.

41. Radicalism: Truth is compatible with, and only compatible with, radicalism.

The truth only finds its home in radicalism. Radicalism adopts a view of human being such that our thinking is always changing and evolving. Radicalism refuses to iconize thinking. Radicalism is thinking and not thought. Radicalism refuses to compromise and is happy in its extremism. Radicalism is philosophy. Radicalism is therefore intellectually promiscuous and believes that where intellectual matters are concerned deflowerings are the flowerings intellectual growth. Radicalism demands constant negotiation with different perspectives. Radicalism entails creativity and self-determination. Radicalism is engagement and ever-more commitment.

Radicalism adopts a view of human being such that our thinking and living is always changing and evolving. .

Because it creates political and social world and because it views thinking as dynamic, radicalism invites doubt any way it turns. "Circles of certainty," as Freire calls them, do not encompass radicalism. Radicalism is open to an evolution of thinking and living.

Radicalism is engagement and ever-more commitment. As the world turns, so does the radical. This is because radicals are engaged in changing the world. The more engaged they become, the more they understand and the more they are committed. Action is requisite for radicalism. Action is the means of testing suppositions and of refining and discarding them.

Does commitment contradict the idea of ever-evolving thinking and living? Is there anything a radical would not be willing to rethink? Would radicals rethink radicalism? I have stated above that radicalism has for its end goal the humanization of all. Is that a dictum that can change, too? What if in our ever-growing commitment we decide that humanization for all is not possible? If radicals always change their minds, can they change their minds on this issue? When I am committed to something, does that mean I become a sectarian? Does commitment to a position (continued humanization of all, for example) mean that I close myself off from other positions? If such is the case, then couldn't we criticize radicalism for circumscribing itself with circles of certainty?

The continued humanization of all people is the universal for radicalism. On that point, and only on that point, it does not question. Commitment is not possible unless some principle is deemed indubitable. Freire never addresses this fundamental problem of radicalism. The moral imperative of radicalism arises in our fellow-feeling toward others and the emergent realization (as we commit ourselves to a greater and greater degree) that oppression must be eliminated. We are reminded of the moral imperative to humanize others only as we are face to face with the oppressed and fellow-feeling is elicited.

In the end, radicalism recognizes commitment only to allowing all people to exercise self-determination. That is the moral imperative of radicalism. The moral imperative arises in fundamental fellow-feeling toward others, which is realized and vivified in our actions and our ever-growing commitment.

Radicalism refuses to iconize. Iconization is inimical to radicalism. Iconization is different from essentials. Iconization is characterized by reverence of an unchanging essence. Essentialism does not mean undying allegiance toward an unchanging essence. It can mean constant revision and rethinking of essence.

Radicalism is intellectually promiscuous. Commitment entails dialoguing with others, allowing ourselves to be changed by what others say. Radicalism never hides from difference. It seeks difference and is committed to understanding the shared humanity underlying all differences. Radicalism is in constant negotiating.

Radicalism believes that deflowering is the means toward flowering. The intellectual promiscuity of radicalism is the deflowering of one perspective and the flowering of another. This deflowering-flowering is the means toward truth. For many, radicalism represents extremism. Philosophers or radicals (there is no difference) are extremists in so much as the object of their inquiry is extreme: Truth. Truth-bearers are extreme for another reason as well: in order to bring out truths and demythicize the world, they must fight against oppressors, who do what they can to prevent the emergence of truth and schooling that encourages people to seek the truth. Truth-bearers cannot succumb to the moderate bureaucrats who want to suppress or gloss over the truth. Their actions to bring forth the truth may have to be extreme (protests, walk-outs, lock-outs), owing to the oppressive system that is endangered by the emergence of such truths.

Radicalism promotes the value of creativity. It must. Radicalism will not allow for the inheritance of tradition. We must create our own beliefs or else we have nothing.

We must create our own beliefs or else we have nothing. The responsibility is on us to create a meaning in our lives. Through our collective efforts, we can build belief systems that reflect our particular world and that best enhance the self-determination of all.

Belief in the creativity of others suggests belief in the ability of others to make their own way, to determine their own lives. Hence, radicalism is not paternalistic. If radicalism is not paternalistic, then it cannot advocate hierarchy in any way. In the classroom the teacher-student relationship is abolished. Nobody talks down to anybody else. Nobody is above anybody else. Radicalism is fundamentally egalitarian.

The democracy of radicalism is not a "democracy" controlled by the elites. It is a democracy that has faith that the majority of people want to participate and can participate in government. Absent from such radicalism is the view that the majority of people are children who must be guided to the water and told to drink it. The majority must be controlled because they need to be controlled. They aren't smart enough to make decisions on their own. They won't take initiative themselves, so somebody must help them. Enter the benevolent ruling class, stage left.

When we engage in dialogue, we seek to negotiate or integrate toward the truth. These negotiations are always good faith negotiations and presuppose truth-telling on the part of all parties. A democracy functions well to the extent that people trust one another, Without a fundamental base of truth-telling, then trust and thus cooperation is not possible.

Radicalism, and only radicalism, is compatible with truth, assuming that truth is dynamic and emerges in process and only in concert with human creativity.

Does radicalism always construe a monster, not a baby, in the bath water? Can I be a radical without wanting to discard the whole system? I answer that in the affirmative, assuming that a baby, not a monster, occupies the bath water. Unlike reform, however, radicalism leaves open the possibility for pervasive and deep changes in a society. Whereas reform rarely sees extremes as plausible, radicalism sees the extremes and that what rests between the extremes. In being able to view the extremes, radicalism points to possibilities at the extremes of the truth spectrum. Reform never considers these possibilities.

Radicalism always questions what kind of kind of being is splashing around in the bath water.

EPILOGUE

Mark Roelof Eleveld

A man stares at the bewildered, angry crowd. Through glasses his eyes are intensely focused, apparently at the faces that surround him. On one wall of the classroom is a cross. On the opposite wall, on the ground in the corner, is a lawn mower, its engine still hot.

The man sees these things, but not as the students, the co-dialoguers see them, at least not initially. He wears a sheet, tied at the shoulder and crossed like a toga, somewhat resembling the garb of Socrates. Behind him, on the wall three photographs hang. He brings them with him to every class, hanging them himself to rid the class of the barren, impersonal university environment. The first, a large poster-like photograph in a golden frame, was given to him by former students, fellow dialoguers. It is a photograph of the wild philosopher, a man not quite six feet tall with sports goggles that seem to raise the height of his graying curly hair into a bunch, as he dribbles the basketball at a former Chicago Bears football player who stands in George's path. The football player dwarfs George, yet the photo reflects George's resolve. Underneath the photo, the caption reads, "You're not the man until you beat the man." The photograph next to it is a little smaller, but just as fascinating. It too is framed in gold, and inside the picture George is seen in spandex, again with goggles, as he is attempting to karate kick a heavy-set man dressed in a robe and wig who is trying with earnest to look like a modern-day Adam Smith. This picture holds no caption, but most of George's students know that it is from the "Great Debate" between George David Miller, AKA Karl Marx, and his long-time nemesis, an economics professor, AKA Adam Smith. By comparison, the third photograph is tame. It shows George's first group of graduate students. They stand in his living room, smiling for the welcoming professor.

Each photograph says a special thing about George, as George has said so many special things about each person. Each moment here is a special one for the enigmatic professor. It is his own strength and energy, coupled together with his overriding compassion for people, that destroys the classroom and creates something greater. The students feed off George, as he feeds off them—together they traverse a path of negotiation and exchange that calls for nothing less then truth toward evaluating value.

"Yeah," shouts the wild-eyed, crazy professor, with spit hanging on his lips as the veins pop out of his neck, "let's talk about environmental issues!" With that, he leaps over desks and in one commanding stroke starts the lawn mower again. Its engine roars through the classroom, down the hallway, and echoes throughout the university. As the sound passes rooms, teachers stop their lectures in mid-sentence and listen, administrators put down their ledgers and listen, and students merely look at one another, as if overcome by the piercing effect of the startling noise. A new sound is in the air of the university, a sound that tastes like liberation and smells of revolution. The sound captures hold of the university. The sound calls for education.

The project George is undertaking is of the greatest importance. He calls for liberation through a revolution of education. What does that mean? What is education? Ignoring the traditional view of education, we can look to the world that surrounds us and see what education truly is.

Not only within the academic canon or within the halls of the university, but within the day-to-day lived world as it occurs—here we find what we learn and how we value. Look at the letter carriers who conceptualize the role of dogs as they have encountered so many critical conflicts with the four-legged beasts. Look at car salespersons who sit across from their customers, playing that familiar game of deceitful negotiation. Look to the alcoholics who sit on their familiar benches, swigging beers to counteract a hangover. This is all part of the educational life that sets the tone for social consciousness and lived evaluation of value.

Every time drivers flip off each other for some petty indiscretion; every time someone spits on another person's lawn; and every time a reluctant sigh is made from a parent toward their child. Each of these cases is a political action that holds specific value. Each of these actions is a motivating factor for recognizing identity. This is the purpose of education. To recognize the political and social developments so as to understand what we value in our lives.

Is this role accurately displayed in an "educational environment?" Does the typical classroom call for these types of evaluation? The simple answer is generally no. So it is George's task, in his latest work, to set up a means for education to do precisely that. His labor is huge. Let us not look at it in any other fashion. It is gigantic. From his own words, "The whole system is rotten to the core and we must come up with a new system to replace it. Because what we have is rotten, we cannot build on it."

In order to see it in a new light, we must again become nomads and pariahs, calling for radicalism toward education. "Radicalism is a commitment to the process of becoming, to the growth and development of individual and social organisms." This is the boulder George casts at the educational edifice. And just as George charged the Chicago Bears football player who stood in his path, so too does George charge the huge traditional pillars that support the rotten myths of education. With the gravity of the subjects George addresses, it would help to set a contextual foundation. The task of deep change is a colossal adventure.

This type of task can be seen under the guise of the revolving governmental politics in the United States, where the fervor of the GOP and the Democratic Party switches hands yearly. Less than five years ago, Clinton danced with his co-reformers to the tune "Don't Stop Thinking About Tomorrow," as flags waved patriotically in the background.

Under the reformation of the new administration, a promising new beginning seemed possible. Three years later, the opposition stood on the hill, waving to the new backlash of government displeasure. Led by Newt Gingrich, the GOP promised the destruction of the reformers, and claiming to reform the reforming. Today and tomorrow would be bright times, according to Gingrich. Today, the roles have switched, and the man dancing on top of the hill is Clinton. The truth is: no role ever switched. Reformers claiming to want reform (Clinton), only to be reformed by someone claiming to reform the reformers (Gingrich), are all the same. No reformation is occurring on either side.

Both sides are molded by the same system, which speaks of reform as a substitute for change. That is why reformation is such a colossal task. It is impossible. Both positions escape the truth, and are forged out of the deceit of the political climate across the United States. No change was ever promised. Reformers merely reformed old words and old promises to new ears. The positions were not contrary, but were the same with superficial ingredients added. Clinton and Gingrich are born of the same mold, a mold promising political inadequacy and social ineptness. This is the system. George says: "Reformers are gradualists. Bit by bit, little by little, things will get better, they say. Evolution, not revolution, they say. Build on what we have, they say. Don't throw the baby out with the bath water, they say." He continues: "Now is the time to throw the baby out with the bath water." He concludes: "Reform gives us false hope that things are really changing for the better."

This is the perspective that George combats. He combats an idea that the system is operable, but needs tweaking. As a radical, he comes from other places to begin revolution.

In 5th century Athens, Aristophanes and other political comic poets were well aware of Socrates prior to his trial and death sentence. He was not hidden in the shadows of the courtyard, or speaking under a pen name as a hidden person. Socrates mocked the Sophists, ridiculed the government, and scorned the leaders of the so-called democratic society. He questioned the core values of his society, searching for the universal values by which to base a just society.

Like Socrates, George says that value is an ontological necessity of life. Value stands at the forefront of any philosophy of education. George and Socrates see ambiguity as a starting point for thinking. The "I know that I do not know" of Socrates can be compared with George's "chaos."

Ambiguity is a necessity for all thinking. Both agree that dialogue is the means for intellectual and spiritual growth. Genuine dialogue is most often aimed at the great edifice of traditions. As radicals, the two want to shake and topple this edifice.

Jesus, too, wanted to topple this great edifice. He saw the evils of Mammon. The greed. The envy. The lust. He overturned the tax tables. George overturns his own tax tables in every sphere of his life. His continuing and emerging dialogue with all of humanity is his method of confronting the evils of the world. He finds intellectual grounding in Socrates, example and inspiration in Jesus, and a contemporary paradigm of education in Paulo Freire.

Freire represents the third part of George's revolutionary triad. The spirit of Freire can be found on every page of *Negotiating Toward Truth*. Not only is deep change possible, but it is possible now! Accommodate not to the status quo, but change the social and political apparatus.

At the 1996 Pedagogy of the Oppressed Conference, Paulo, frail and old, began to speak to the large audience. He looked uncomfortable being in a role that was more impersonal than what his philosophy represented. In front of stood a large podium, an indirect symbol of what he had fought against his whole life. The revolution could not be enacted in this setting. Thus, before he began, he asked for the podium to be moved, to be toppled, so that we could speak as we should, with nothing between us.

It was a small moment, but a large metaphor of his life and work. I associate George with this moment. Each time he steps into a dialogue, engaging in exchange and negotiation, he topples some structure that separates him from his students. He talks with, not against, other people in the class. He provides leadership and insight into the revolution by being a radical and nurturing a caring liberatory education that rests on "having differences" and not "being different."

We must seek each other out. We must become pariahs and nomads in search of answers. George offers a compelling message in *Negotiating Toward Truth*. But from my perspective, his living example offers a greater example of the fulfillment of that message.

We are not in a time to watch the glory of Socrates as he tempts the authors of democracy to question their own virtue. We are not at a time to witness the young bearded Jesus stand against injustice as he kicks over the evils that are destroying humanity. We are no longer in a time to talk to the man who was exiled for liberating the minds of peasants. We are in a troubled time where George offers a message that applies to our neighbors, our family, our co-workers, and our lovers. Human beings always have time to control their own destinies. The first step is to become a radical.

A Poem: Of philosophers and all

Philosophers listen, hear, and try to convey
And all that is in the heart of words
Is all that is in the heart of those around them.
To come together is to create art—
To come together is to create history—
To come together is poetry.

NOTES

Introduction

1. Paulo Freire, *Pedagogy of the Oppressed*, trans. Myra Bergman Ramos (New York: Continuum, 1970, 1993), p. 53.
2. John Dewey, *John Dewey on Education: Selected Writings*, ed. Reginald D. Archambault (New York: The Modern Library, 1964), pp. 427-430.
3. George David Miller and Conrad P. Pritscher, *On Education and Values: In Praise of Pariahs and Nomads* (Amsterdam and Atlanta: Rodopi, 1995).
4. John Dewey, *Philosophy of Education (Problems of Men)* (Totowa, N.J.: Littlefield, Adams, & Co., 1958), pp. 5-6.
5. *Ibid.*, p. 10.

Chapter One: Nietzsche's Treatment of Becoming

1. Friedrich Nietzsche, *On the Advantage and Disadvantage of History for Life*, trans., with an Introduction by Peter Preuss (Indianapolis, Ind: Hackett, 1980), pp. 8-10.
2. *Ibid.*, p. 55.
3. Friedrich Nietzsche, *Thus Spoke Zarathustra*, in *The Portable Nietzsche*, ed. and trans. Walter Kaufmann (New York: Penguin Books, 1954), pp. 137-141.
4. Nietzsche, *On the Advantage and Disadvantage of History for Life*, p. 64.
5. Paulo Freire, *Pedagogy of the Oppressed*, trans. Myra Bergman Ramos (New York: Continuum, 1970, 1993), pp. 17-18
6. Friedrich Nietzsche, *The Will to Power*, trans. Walter Kaufmann and R.J. Hollingdale, ed. Walter Kaufmann (New York: Vintage, 1968), p. 330.
7. Nietzsche, *Twilight of the Idols*, in *The Portable Nietzsche*, pp. 473-474.
8. Freire, *Pedagogy of the Oppressed*, p. 30.
9. Friedrich Nietzsche, *The Gay Science*, trans. Walter Kaufmann (New York: Vintage, 1970), pp. 327-331.
10. George David Miller and Conrad P. Pritscher, *On Education and Values: In Praise of Pariahs and Nomads* (Amsterdam and Atlanta: Rodopi, 1995), p. 25.
11. Nietzsche, *The Will to Power*, pp. 274-275.

Chapter Two: The Inert Ideas of Alfred North Whitehead

1. Martin Luther King, Jr., "Letter from Birmingham City Jail," in *A Testament of Hope*, ed. James M. Washington (San Francisco: Harper Collins, 1986), p. 296.
2. Alfred North Whitehead, *The Aims of Education and Other Essays* (New York: The Free Press, 1929), p. v.
3. *Ibid.*, p. 1.
4. Friedrich Nietzsche, *Thus Spoke Zarathustra* in *The Portable Nietzsche*, ed. and trans. Walter Kaufmann (New York: Penguin Books, 1954), pp. 137-141.

5. Whitehead, *The Aims of Education and Other Essays*, p. 2.

6. Frantz Fanon, *Wretched of the Earth*, trans. Constance Farrington, Preface by Jean-Paul Sartre (New York: Grove Press, 1963), p. 38.

7. Whitehead, *The Aims of Education and Other Essays*, p. 6.

8. Alfred North Whitehead, *Science and the Modern World* (New York: The Free Press, 1925), pp. 198-199.

9. *Ibid.*, p. 199.

10. *Ibid.*, pp., 199-200.

11. Imanuel Kant, *Critique of Pure Reason*, trans. Norman Kemp Smith (London: Macmillan, 1956), p. 93.

12. Whitehead, *Science and the Modern World*, p. 200.

13. Whitehead, *The Aims of Education and Other Essays*, pp. 6-7.

14. William James, "The Will To Believe," in *The Writings of William James*, ed. John J. McDermott (New York: The Modern Library, 1968), pp. 717-735.

15. Whitehead, *The Aims of Education and Other Essays*, p. 12.

16. George David Miller and Conrad P. Pritscher, *On Education and Values: In Praise of Pariahs and Nomads* (Amsterdam and Atlanta: Rodopi, 1995).

17. Whitehead, *The Aims of Education and Other Essays*, p. 29.

18. *Ibid.*

19. *Ibid.*, p. 30.

20. *Ibid.*

21. *Ibid.*, p. 32.

22. George David Miller, Editorial Foreword to *The Human Project and the Temptations of Science* by Lansana Keita (Amsterdam and Atlanta: Rodopi, forthcoming), pp. vii-viii.

23. Whitehead, *The Aims of Educaton and Other Essays*, p. 30.

24. Friedrich Nietzsche, *The Birth of Tragedy*, in *The Birth of Tragedy and The Case of Wagner*, trans., with a commentary by Walter Kaufmann (New York: Vintage, 1967), pp. 33-72.

25. Whitehead, *The Aims of Education and Other Essays*, pp. 32-33.

26. Paulo Freire, *Pedagogy of the Oppressed*, trans. Myra Bergman Ramos (New York: Continuum, 1970, 1993), p. 57.

27. David Hume, *An Inquiry Concerning Human Understanding*, ed. with an introduction by Charles W. Hendel (Indianapolis, Ind: Bobbs Merrill , 1955), p. 19.

28. Whitehead, *The Aims of Educaton and Other Essays*, p. 37.

29. *Ibid.*, p. 25.

30. *Ibid.*, p. 28.

31. *Ibid.*, pp. 19, 28.

32. *Ibid.*, p. 37.

33. *Ibid.*, p. 96.

34. *Ibid.*, p. 98.

35. Whitehead, *Science and the Modern World*, p. 18.

36. *Ibid.*, pp. 196, 202-203.

37. Whitehead, *The Aims of Educaton and Other Essays*, p. 121.

38. *Ibid.*, p. 151.

39. *Ibid.*, pp. 30, 32.

40. Whitehead, *Science and the Modern World*, p. 207.
41. *Ibid.*, p. 202.

Chapter Three: Upgrading Dewey

1. John Dewey, *Moral Principles of Education* (New York: The Wisdom Library, 1959), p. 55.
2. John Dewey, *How We Think* (Boston: D.C. Heath & Co., 1910), p. 201.
3. Dewey, *Moral Principles of Education*, p. 2.
4. *Ibid.*, p. 10.
5. *Ibid.*, pp. 52-53.
6. *Ibid.*, p. 33.
7. John Dewey, *John Dewey On Education*, ed. Reginald D. Archambault (New York: The Modern Library, 1964), pp. 249-254.
8. *Ibid.*, p. 253.
9. Dewey, *How We Think*, p. 130.
10. *Ibid.*, p. 3.
11. *Ibid.*, p. 40.
12. *Ibid.*
13. *Ibid.*
14. *Ibid.*
15. *Ibid.*
16. *Ibid.*, p. 2.
17. *Ibid.*, p. 130.
18. John Dewey, *Philosophy of Education (Problems of Men)* (Totowa, N.J.: Littlefield, Adams, & Co., 1958), pp. 3-20.
19. Jean-Paul Sartre, *Being and Nothingness: A Phenomenological Essay on Ontology*, trans. Hazel Barnes (New York: Washington Square Books, 1956).
20. Dewey, *John Dewey on Education*, p. 4.
21. *Ibid.*, p. 430.
22. *Ibid.*, p. 432.
23. Martin Luther King, Jr., *A Testament of Hope*, ed. James M. Washington (San Francisco: Harper Collins, 1986), pp. 14-15.
24. Paulo Freire, *Pedagogy of the Oppressed*, trans. Myra Bergman Ramos (New York: Continuum, 1970, 1993), pp. 52-67.
25. Dewey, *John Dewey on Education*, p. 425.
26. *Ibid.*
27. Dewey, *How We Think*, pp. 138-139.
28. Dewey, *John Dewey on Education*, pp. 219-220.
29. *Ibid.*, p. 249.
30. *Ibid.*, p. 257.
31. Freire, *Pedagogy of the Oppressed*, pp. 17-18.
32. Dewey, *How We Think*, p. 136.
33. *Ibid.*, pp. 142-143.
34. *Ibid.*, p. 137.
35. *Ibid.*, p. 138.

36. *Ibid.,* p. 139.
37. *Ibid.,* p. 149.

Chapter Four: Freire's Radicalism

1. Paulo Freire, *Pedagogy of the Oppressed,* trans. Myra Bergman Ramos (New York: Continuum, 1970, 1993), pp. 17-22.
2. *Ibid.,* p. 18.
3. *Ibid.,* p. 20.
4. *Ibid.,* p. 18.
5. *Ibid.,* p. 19.
6. *Ibid.,* pp. 20-21.
7. *Ibid.,* p. 25-26.
8. *Ibid.,* p. 66.
9. *Ibid.,* p. 26.
10. G.W.F. Hegel, *Phenomenology of Spirit,* trans. A.V. Miller, with an Analysis and Foreword by J.N. Findlay (Oxford: Oxford University Press, 1977), pp. 111-119.
11. Freire, *Pedagogy of the Oppressed,* p. 41.
12. *Ibid.,* p. 73.
13. *Ibid.*
14. Søren Kierkegaard, *The Sickness Unto Death,* trans. Walter Lowrie, p. 163; quoted by Ernest Becker, *The Denial of Death* (New York and London: The Free Press, 1973), p. 72.
15. Friedrich Nietzsche, *The Birth of Tragedy,* in *The Birth of Tragedy and The Case of Wagner,* trans., with a commentary by Walter Kaufmann (New York: Vintage, 1967), p. 60.
16. Freire, *Pedagogy of the Oppressed,* p. 87.
17. Jean-Paul Sartre, *Being and Nothingness,* trans. Hazel Barnes (New York: Washington Square Press, 1956), p. 122.
18. Paulo Freire, "Pedagogy of the Oppressed Conference," Omaha, Nebraska (22 March 1996).
19. Freire, *Pedagogy of the Oppressed,* p. 52.
20. *Ibid.,* p. 54.
21. Martin Luther King, Jr., *A Testament of Hope,* ed. James M. Washington (San Francisco: Harper Collins, 1986), pp. 14-15.
22. Paulo Freire, *Pedagogy of the Oppressed,* pp. 60-61.
23. *Ibid.,* p. 62.
24. *Ibid.,* p. 65.
25. *Ibid.,* p. 72.
26. Shulamith Firestone, *The Dialectic of Sex: The Case for Feminist Revolution* (New York: William Morrow, 1970), p. 99.
27. Paulo Freire, *Pedagogy of the Oppressed,* pp. 77-105.
28. *Ibid.,* p. 86.
29. *Ibid.,* p. 90.
30. *Ibid.,* pp. 91-105.

31. *Ibid.*, pp. 26-27.
32. King, *A Testament of Hope*, p. 323.
33. Freire, *Pedagogy of the Oppressed*, p. 36.
34. Freire, *A Testament of Hope*, p. 323.
35. Freire, *Pedagogy of the Oppressed*, p. 29.
36. *Ibid.*, p. 30.
37. *Ibid.*, pp. 68-73.
38. *Ibid.*, p. 68.
39. Immanuel Kant, *Lectures on Ethics*, trans. Louis Infield, Foreword by Lewis White Beck (Indianapolis, Ind: Hackett, 1963), p. 224.
40. Freire, *Pedagogy of the Oppressed*, p. 69.
41. *Ibid.*, p. 71.
42. *Ibid.*, p. 73.
43. *Ibid.*, pp. 122-123.
44. *Ibid.*, p. 20.
45. *Ibid.*, p. 32.
46. *Ibid.*, p. 68.
47. *Ibid.*, pp. 122-123.
48. *Ibid.*, p. 124.
49. *Ibid.*
50. *Ibid.*, p. 125.
51. *Ibid.*, p. 129.
52. *Ibid.*, p. 131.
53. *Ibid.*, p. 141
54. *Ibid.*, p. 120.

Chapter Five: A Radical Pedagogical Creed of Dynamism

1. Jean-Paul Sartre, *Being and Nothingness*, trans. Hazel Barnes (New York: Washington Square Press, 1956), p. 122.
2. Martin Luther King, Jr., *A Testament of Hope*, ed. James M. Washington (San Francisco: Harper Collins, 1986), p. 123.
3. George David Miller and Conrad P. Pritscher, *On Education and Values: In Praise of Pariahs and Nomads* (Amsterdam and Atlanta: Rodopi, 1996), pp. 25-55.
4. Noam Chomsky, *Necessary Illusions: Thought Control in Democratic Societies* (Boston: South End Press, 1989), p. 24.
5. Karl Marx, *The Portable Karl Marx*, ed. Eugene Kamenka (New York: Penguin, 1983), pp. 136-141.
6. Adapted from George David Miller and Mark Roelof Eleveld, "'Having Differences' and 'Being Different': From a Dialogue of Difference to the Private Language of Indifference," *Researcher*, 11 (December 1996), pp. 51-56.
7. G.W.F. Hegel, *Phenomenology of Spirit*, trans. A.V. Miller (Oxford: Oxford University Press, 1977), p. 38.
8. *Ibid.*, p. 121
9. Sarah Lucia Hoagland, *Lesbian Ethics: Toward New Value* (Palo Alto, Cal: Institute of Lesbian Studies, 1992), p. 159.

10. Freire, *Pedagogy of the Oppressed*, p. 129.

11. Hegel, *Phenomenology of Spirit*, pp. 221-228.

12. Hoagland, *Lesbian Ethics*, p. 133.

13. W.E.B. DuBois, *W.E.B. DuBois: A Reader*, ed. David Levering Lewis (New York: Henry Holt and Company, 1995), p. 559.

14. King, *A Testament of Hope*, p .502.

15. Hoagland, *Lesbian Ethics*, p. 221.

16. Hegel, *Phenomenology of Spirit*, p. 69.

17. *Ibid.*, p. 68.

18. *Ibid.*, pp. 68-69.

19. *Ibid.*, p. 73.

BIBLIOGRAPHY

Chomsky, Noam. *Necessary Illusions: Thought Control in Democratic Socities*. Boston: South End Press, 1989.

Dewey, John *Dewey on Education: Selections*.With an Introduction and Notes by Martin S. Dworkin. New York: Teacher's College Press, 1959.

____. *How We Think*. Boston: D.C. Heath & Co., 1910.

____. *John Dewey on Education: Selected Writings*. Ed. Reginald D. Archambault. New York: The Modern Library, 1964.

____. *Moral Principles in Education*. New York: Philosophical Library, Inc., 1959.

____. *Philosophy of Education (Problems of Men)*. Totowa, N.J.: Littlefield, Adams & Co., 1966.

Firestone, Shulamith. *The Dialectic of Sex: The Case for Feminist Revolution*: New York: William Morrow, 1970.

Freire, Paulo. *Pedagogy of the Oppressed*. Newly Revised 20th-Anniversary Edition. Trans. Myra Bergman Ramos. New York: Continuum, 1970, 1993.

Hegel, G.W.F. *Phenomenology of Spirit*. Trans. A.V. Miller. With Analysis of the Text and Foreword by J.N. Findlay. Oxford: Oxford University Press, 1977.

James, William. "The Will to Believe." In *The Writings of William James*. Ed. John J. McDermott. New York: The Modern Library, 1967.

King, Martin Luther, Jr. *A Testament of Hope: The Essential Writings and Speeches of Martin Luther King, Jr*. Ed. James Melvin Washington. San Francisco: Harper Collins, 1986

Miller, George David. *An Idiosyncratic Ethics; Or, the Lauramachean Ethics*. Amsterdam and Atlanta: Rodopi, 1994.

____. "Open-Mindedness and Muddled Minds: Fusion in Confusion." *The Journal of Value Inquiry*, 30 (June 1996), pp. 63-80.

Miller, George David and Conrad P. Pritscher. *On Education and Values: In Praise of Pariahs and Nomads*. Amsterdam and Atlanta: Rodopi, 1995.

Nietzsche, Friedrich. *Untimely Meditations*. Trans. R.J. Hollingdale. New York: Cambridge University Press, 1992

____. *The Will to Power*. Trans. Walter Kaufmann and R.J. Hollingdale. Ed. Walter
    Kaufmann. New York: Vintage, 1968.

Sartre, Jean-Paul. *Being and Nothingness: A Phenomenological Essay on Ontology*.
    Trans. Hazel Barnes. New York: Washington Square Press Books, 1956.

Whitehead, Alfred North. *Adventures of Ideas*. New York: Macmillan, 1933.

____. *The Aims of Education and Other Essays*. New York: The Free Press, 1929.

____. *Science and the Modern World*. New York: The Free Press, 1925.

ABOUT THE AUTHOR

George David Miller teaches philosophy at Lewis University in Romeoville, Illinois, where he is graduate director of the Master of Arts Program in Philosophy and Director of the Scholars Program. Miller serves as an Associate Editor of the Value Inquiry Book Series (VIBS); as Editor of the VIBS Philosophy of Education Special Series; and as a member of the VIBS Executive Board. His publications include: *An Idiosyncratic Ethics; Or the Lauramachean Ethics* (Rodopi, 1994) and (with Conrad P. Pritscher) *On Education and Values: In Praise of Pariahs and Nomads* (Rodopi, 1995), which was nominated for the 1996 Grawemeyer Award in Education. In October 1997, the Council For Advancement and Support of Education selected Miller as the 1997 Carnegie Foundation for the Advancement of Teaching Illinois Professor of the Year.

INDEX

INDEX

INDEX

INDEX

VIBS

The **Value Inquiry Book Series** is co-sponsored by:

American Maritain Association
American Society for Value Inquiry
Association for Personalist Studies
Association for Process Philosophy of Education
Center for East European Dialogue and Development, Rochester Institute of
Technology
Centre for Cultural Research, Aarhus University
College of Education and Allied Professions, Bowling Green State University
Concerned Philosophers for Peace
Conference of Philosophical Societies
International Academy of Philosophy of the Principality of Liechtenstein
International Society for Universalism
Natural Law Society
Philosophical Society of Finland
Philosophy Born of Struggle Association
Philosophy Seminar, University of Mainz
R.S. Hartman Institute for Formal and Applied Axiology
Society for Iberian and Latin-American Thought
Society for the Philosophic Study of Genocide and the Holocaust
Society for the Philosophy of Sex and Love
Yves R. Simon Institute.

Titles Published

1. Noel Balzer, *The Human Being as a Logical Thinker.*

2. Archie J. Bahm, *Axiology: The Science of Values.*

3. H. P. P. (Hennie) Lötter, *Justice for an Unjust Society.*

4. H. G. Callaway, *Context for Meaning and Analysis: A Critical Study in the Philosophy of Language.*

5. Benjamin S. Llamzon, *A Humane Case for Moral Intuition.*

6. James R. Watson, *Between Auschwitz and Tradition: Postmodern Reflections on the Task of Thinking.* A volume in **Holocaust and Genocide Studies.**

7. Robert S. Hartman, *Freedom to Live: The Robert Hartman Story,* edited by Arthur R. Ellis. A volume in **Hartman Institute Axiology Studies.**

8. Archie J. Bahm, *Ethics: The Science of Oughtness.*

9. George David Miller, *An Idiosyncratic Ethics; Or, the Lauramachean Ethics.*

10. Joseph P. DeMarco, *A Coherence Theory in Ethics.*

11. Frank G. Forrest, *Valuemetrics: The Science of Personal and Professional Ethics.* A volume in **Hartman Institute Axiology Studies.**

12. William Gerber, *The Meaning of Life: Insights of the World's Great Thinkers.*

13. Richard T. Hull, Editor, *A Quarter Century of Value Inquiry: Presidential Addresses of the American Society for Value Inquiry.* A volume in **Histories and Addresses of Philosophical Societies.**

14. William Gerber, *Nuggets of Wisdom from Great Jewish Thinkers: From Biblical Times to the Present.*

30. Robin Attfield, *Value, Obligation, and Meta-Ethics.*

31. William Gerber, *The Deepest Questions You Can Ask About God: As Answered by the World's Great Thinkers.*

32. Daniel Statman, *Moral Dilemmas.*

33. Rem B. Edwards, Editor, *Formal Axiology and Its Critics.* A volume in **Hartman Institute Axiology Studies.**

34. George David Miller and Conrad P. Pritscher, *On Education and Values: In Praise of Pariahs and Nomads.* A volume in **Philosophy of Education.**

35. Paul S. Penner, *Altruistic Behavior: An Inquiry into Motivation.*

36. Corbin Fowler, *Morality for Moderns.*

37. Giambattista Vico, *The Art of Rhetoric (Institutiones Oratoriae,* 1711-1741), from the definitive Latin text and notes, Italian commentary and introduction by Giuliano Crifò, translated and edited by Giorgio A. Pinton and Arthur W. Shippee. A volume in **Values in Italian Philosophy.**

38. W. H. Werkmeister, *Martin Heidegger on the Way,* edited by Richard T. Hull. A volume in **Werkmeister Studies.**

39. Phillip Stambovsky, *Myth and the Limits of Reason.*

40. Samantha Brennan, Tracy Isaacs, and Michael Milde, Editors, *A Question of Values: New Canadian Perspectives in Ethics and Political Philosophy.*

41. Peter A. Redpath, *Cartesian Nightmare: An Introduction to Transcendental Sophistry.* A volume in **Studies in the History of Western Philosophy.**

42. Clark Butler, *History as the Story of Freedom: Philosophy in Intercultural Context,* with Responses by sixteen scholars.

43. Dennis Rohatyn, *Philosophy History Sophistry.*

44. Leon Shaskolsky Sheleff, *Social Cohesion and Legal Coercion: A Critique of Weber, Durkheim, and Marx.* Afterword by Virginia Black.

45. Alan Soble, Editor, *Sex, Love, and Friendship: Studies of the Society for the Philosophy of Sex and Love, 1977-1992.* A volume in **Histories and Addresses of Philosophical Societies.**

46. Peter A. Redpath, *Wisdom's Odyssey: From Philosophy to Transcendental Sophistry.* A volume in **Studies in the History of Western Philosophy.**

47. Albert A. Anderson, *Universal Justice: A Dialectical Approach.* A volume in **Universal Justice.**

48. Pio Colonnello, *The Philosophy of José Gaos.* Translated from Italian by Peter Cocozzella. Edited by Myra Moss. Introduction by Giovanni Gullace. A volume in **Values in Italian Philosophy.**

49. Laura Duhan Kaplan and Laurence F. Bove, Editors, *Philosophical Perspectives on Power and Domination: Theories and Practices.* A volume in **Philosophy of Peace.**

50. Gregory F. Mellema, *Collective Responsibility.*

51. Josef Seifert, *What Is Life? The Originality, Irreducibility, and Value of Life.* A volume in **Central-European Value Studies.**

52. William Gerber, *Anatomy of What We Value Most.*

53. Armando Molina, *Our Ways: Values and Character,* edited by Rem B. Edwards. A volume in **Hartman Institute Axiology Studies.**

54. Kathleen J. Wininger, *Nietzsche's Reclamation of Philosophy.* A volume in **Central-European Value Studies.**

55. Thomas Magnell, Editor, *Explorations of Value.*

56. HPP (Hennie) Lötter, *Injustice, Violence, and Peace: The Case of South Africa.* A volume in **Philosophy of Peace.**

57. Lennart Nordenfelt, *Talking About Health: A Philosophical Dialogue.* A volume in **Nordic Value Studies.**

58. Jon Mills and Janusz A. Polanowski, *The Ontology of Prejudice.* A volume in **Philosophy and Psychology.**

59. Leena Vilkka, *The Intrinsic Value of Nature*.

60. Palmer Talbutt, Jr., *Rough Dialectics: Sorokin's Philosophy of Value*, with Contributions by Lawrence T. Nichols and Pitirim A. Sorokin.

61. C. L. Sheng, *A Utilitarian General Theory of Value*.

62. George David Miller, *Negotiating Toward Truth: The Extinction of Teachers and Students*. Epilogue by Mark Roelof Eleveld. A volume in **Philosophy of Education.**

www.ingramcontent.com/pod-product-compliance
Lightning Source LLC
Chambersburg PA
CBHW020354270326
41926CB00007B/434